Sonnets

SONNETS

150 CONTEMPORARY SONNETS

Edited By
William Baer

University of Evansville Press
Evansville, Indiana

The text of this book is composed in Times New Roman.
Composition by Creative Press.
Manufacturing by Thomson-Shore.
Book and Cover Design: W.B.

Library of Congress Cataloging-in-Publication Data

Sonnets: 150 contemporary sonnets / edited by William Baer. — 1st ed.
    p. cm.
  ISBN 0-930982-59-2
  1. Sonnets, American. 2. American poetry—20th century. 3. American
poetry — 21st century. I. Baer, William, 1948-

PS593.S6S59 2005
811'.04208054—dc22

                                        2004055396

Acknowledgments and copyright notice for individual poems begin on
page 173.

The University of Evansville Press
1800 Lincoln Avenue
Evansville, IN 47722
(812)479-2963

For my family and friends

CONTENTS

Introduction

The sonnet is one of the greatest human inventions, and it has provided the format for some of humanity's greatest works of art. Its rigorously-rhymed fourteen metrical lines are a perfection of form that allows for endless variation. The sonnet is like a faceted diamond, or a snowflake (always a hexagon), or a baseball diamond, or a chessboard set with its thirty-two pieces. All are highly structured, and each provides the basis for infinite beauty, excitement, and possibility.

Ever since the first sonnet appeared in Italy in the 13th Century (a gift from Apollo according to J. L. Borges in his sonnet "*Un Poeta del Siglo XIII*"), the little *sonetto* has enjoyed tremendous popularity in many countries and in most time periods (see appendix, "A Brief History of the Sonnet," page 153). In the English language, the sonnet has been used by almost all of our greatest poets, including Spenser, Shakespeare, Milton, Donne, Wordsworth, Shelley, Keats, and Tennyson. Even in the "experimental" 20th Century, many of the world's most renowned poets have used the demanding sonnet format: Yeats, Valéry, Frost, Rilke, Machado, Lorca, Borges, Neruda, and Auden. Even the radical experimenter Ezra Pound claimed to have written hundreds of sonnets, and T. S. Eliot incorporated two back-to-back English sonnets in "The Fire Sermon" section of *The Waste Land*.

Nevertheless, in the late 1960's, a number of writers in the United States, in an effort to exhibit their "*au courant*" thinking, declared that the sonnet was dead. A popular derision was Robert Bly's comment that "The sonnet is where old professors go to die," and, much more sadly, William Carlos Williams' absurd remark that the sonnet was somehow "Fascist" — which surely would have surprised Lorca and Neruda. For over twenty-five years, the sonnet was generally abused and ignored in America, and it appeared less and less in the literary journals. During this period, certain established poets continued to write excellent sonnets — like Richard Wilbur, Howard Nemerov, Anthony Hecht, England's Philip Larkin, and others — but the prevailing *Weltanschauung* was definitely anti-sonnet.

Then in the 1980's, many younger poets began to write in formal modes again. This formalist revival, initiated by the talented but misnamed New Formalists, laid the groundwork for the current revival of the sonnet. As a result, contemporary poets have discovered that the most "modern" and "contemporary" thoughts and feelings can be powerfully conveyed within the tightly-structured format of the sonnet, and this anthology contains a selection of work from this exciting new literary trend.

Fortunately, many of the mainline literary journals are now publishing sonnets again, and there are now several websites dedicated exclusively to the sonnet. From 1994-2000, Felix Stefanile published his excellent annual, *The Yearbook of the Sonnet*, and the poetry journal *The Formalist* (which I edit) has published hundreds of sonnets since our inaugural issue in Spring/Summer 1990 — especially in conjunction with our annual Howard Nemerov Sonnet Competition, which was initiated in 1994. In more recent years, a number of poets, in the tradition of Shakespeare, Elizabeth Browning, and Edna St. Vincent Millay, have begun to publish entire collections of sonnets, such as Harold Witt's *American Lit* (1994), Marilyn Hacker's *Love, Death, and the Changing of the Seasons* (1995), Willis Barnstone's *The Secret Reader* (1996), Ronald Wallace's *The Uses of Adversity* (1998), Robert Daseler's *Levering Avenue* (1998), Mark Jarman's *Unholy Sonnets* (2000), and my own *"Borges" and Other Sonnets* (2003) — and more sonnet collections are on the way (from Tony Barnstone, Greg Williamson, and others).

The sonnets included in this anthology showcase a wide range of poets, from a recipient of the Nobel Prize to younger writers who are just beginning to appear in the literary journals. The selection includes many of the editor's favorite contemporary sonnets from the past fifteen years, but it hardly claims to be comprehensive. At *The Formalist* alone, we've published over five hundred talented sonneteers. As for the poems themselves, with few exceptions, the sonnets included in this anthology were written in strict rhymed formats with mostly solid rhymes. Most of the sonnets were also composed in either the standard English or Italian rhyme schemes, but there are numerous variations as well.

I would like to take this opportunity to thank my wife, Mona, whose work at *The Formalist* has done so much to promote the contemporary sonnet. I'm also very grateful to Maureen Duncan for her help in preparing this manuscript.

The sonnet is back, and it's right where it should be — at the center of attention. I hope you'll enjoy this sampling.

— William Baer

"Scorn not the sonnet . . ."

— Wordsworth

DANIEL ANDERSON

Standard Time

The church's spire, the courthouse clock,
And all the slanted roofs that line the square,
Of dime store, bank, and Mitchell's Shoe Repair,
Have joined their silhouettes to interlock
Against the evening's cold cornflower sky.
The velvet counter-darkness of the street
Seems painted by the sly hand of Magritte
To stump the mind and its bewildered eye.

A failing light. The growing zodiac.
A windfall hour spent. Each leaf-lined yard
Is cloaked in tones of cobblestone and slate
As we discover in our turning back
An early dusk we cannot disregard,
A change we never quite anticipate.

Original Sin

When they conspired, whispering on the phone
With racing hearts, to meet for drinks that day
At a dark, romantic, byzantine cafe
In a neighborhood where they would not be known,
They could not know its gravity, or the sighs,
The tears, the degradations now to come —
The neon mean motels; becoming numb
To conscience, bold at telling teeny lies
That smolder in the gut; the grim mutations
In relations till a look, like a pebble loosed,
Will start an avalanche, or a spark produced
By a casual word ignite a conflagration.
A cosmos can be undone by acts as small
As eating an apple, or observing one fall.

Fog

On the densest days, he guides his little boat
into the heart of the fog, turns off the key,
lies on the deck, and lets her float,
drifting sightless over the gentle sea,
into that all-consuming whitish-grey
of the fog, into its palpable negation,
into its wets and damps, drifting away
into its gradual world of obliteration,
where nothing-at-all exists except
the solipsism, which, in time, will bring
him to the essence of himself: swept
away, a blank, devoid of everything,
except the thought of you, and of your death,
enshrouded in mist as moist as your final breath.

Snowflake

Timing's everything. The vapor rises
high in the sky, tossing to and fro,
then freezes, suddenly, and crystallizes
into a perfect flake of miraculous snow.
For countless miles, drifting east above
the world, whirling about in a swirling free-
for-all, appearing aimless, just like love,
but sensing, seeking-out, its destiny.
Falling to where the two young skaters stand,
hand in hand, then flips and dips and whips
itself about to ever-so-gently land,
a miracle, across her unkissed lips:
as he blocks the wind raging from the south,
leaning forward to kiss her lovely mouth.

Adam

(Gen 4:8)

He'd seen this thing before, of course, but never
like this. After Eden, he'd found a swan
lying motionless and silent, forever
rotting, irretrievable, and gone.
But now, it's his boy, the brother of Cain,
the shepherd son, the kind and faithful friend
of He-Who-Is, lying quiet and slain:
finished, futureless, at the end of his end.
Once, Adam had named the names, and named his own
two sons, and named this curse, which nullifies
and terminates, as "death." But he who'd known
the awesome power of God looked to the skies,
knowing, without a doubt, though nothing was said,
his God both could and would undo the dead.

LISA BARNETT

To a Mismatched Pair: A Valentine

The teenaged couple waiting for the train
must be in love or think they are, although
his arms are not quite long enough to go
around her broad expanse and they're both plain:
graceless, with bad teeth, bad skin. Still, they remain,
their bodies locked in the imperfect O
of their embrace. Uncharmed by their bold show,
we look at them and look away again.

But what if they were beautiful? We'd look
and find their love a lovely thing: no flaw
would hide the content of their hearts or draw
our eyes away from such an open book
— as though we thought a photo-op emotion
could be the only measure of devotion.

Arithmetic

Two eyes, one nose, one mouth, and what could be
more perfect? Maybe the small fraction of
a smile she aims at his glance secretly
across the living room, a cryptic love
that no one else divines, and later in
the loft their silent battle not to wake
his friend down on the couch who snores as thin
strained cries rain down. Maybe the way they take
the root of self, forgetting *mine* and *yours,*
and add one body to another, blue
sensation multiplied. Maybe this score,
arithmetic of love they do as years
subtract themselves yet strangely add up to
how many, and how much, and to much more.

Audit

The time has come he never thought would come
when he sees her see in him just defects.
As if his love is what has kept her down,
what once she thought was perfect she rejects.
She takes an audit of his qualities,
subtracts affection, multiplies distress,
and so, in sum, she takes his sum and sees
the countless reasons she should need him less.
She knows him better than he knows himself
so if she finds his love to be oppression,
and reads these years of joy as years of lies,
then he must turn his mind against himself
and see, laid out in infinite regression,
his net and gross of failure in her eyes.

WILLIS BARNSTONE

Wang Wei and Snow

Although Wang Wei is peaceful looking at
the apricot, the sea gull and the frost
climbing the village hills, or feels the mat
of pine trees on the mountain sky, or lost
in meditation loses nature and
the outer light and sings his way through mist
inside, although Wang Wei becomes the land
and loitering rain, his mountain clouds exist
in poems — not in life — and turn like mills
never exhausting time. Wang Wei also
was stuck in life, and from his hermitage
he tells a friend to walk the idle hills
alone, to swallow failure like the age-
ing year, to dream (what else is there?) of snow.

If I Could Phone the Soul

The night is beautiful. I live alone
and hope. It's better than to be the king
of rainy nations. Yet if I could phone
the soul, my soul, your soul, or see my being,
if I could sleep outside of time a while
and know why I am ticking toward a sleep
where time will fail (at least for me), I'd smile.
I smile right now, which means I groan, I creep
with shame because I'll always be a fool.
The night is beautiful. I pray. I lie.
I love. I'm happy. Everyone is poor,
especially the king of rain whose rule
drops me dead on a moon where I can't die.
I'm stupid. Love is you. We have no cure.

Sirens

Sirens are singing monsters of the sea
who live on mountains in the north. A bridge
connects two peaks, and from that height I see
their yellow eyes: star beacons on the ridge,
longing to shake me into the abyss.
Their passion fills my ears. I've thrown away
the wax, and despite trembling cowardice
I hear the river in their throats. My way
is clear. Their fatal weapon is my choice.
The singing pierces the protective fan
of lead under my clothes. Their wings explode
like virtue cracking through a Puritan.
Easy as consciousness, I jump, a toad
into the waters of their cloudy voice.

Sonnet: Detective Work

We know the man should not have drowned tonight.
We know this from the way his head was turned
upward, the gash, the bloody towels. We learned
this from his sad expression. Oh, he *might*
have slipped on the tile floor. What do we know?
We know this much. He was alive to fill
the tub. And something else. He wasn't ill.
It's even said he had someplace to go
tonight. His wife told us about the play,
the dinner reservations. If he drowned
at all tonight, it could be that she found
him on the baby-sitter Saturday
a week ago. One must suspect the spouse,
but most accidents happen in the house.

Going to See **Casablanca***: 1945*

To walk for the last time past the square
And down to the theater below the hill;
To search your eyes and touch your yellow hair
And wonder at my curious lack of will;
To think how all the spring we strolled about,
Learning the solid flesh we did not know,
But on this final night I take you out
To view the phantoms of a picture show.

Is it because, as in the airport scene
When stoic Bogart puts first things first,
I know the war is going to intervene
And all our small arrangements be dispersed,
And love be tested, and its truth be told,
That I am so preoccupied and cold?

No Doubt?

A healthy skepticism is, no doubt
(See how a pun can lend to paradox),
An asset in a world of claims. Without
It, one's a goose and prey to every fox
The woods can hold. To not end up their feast,
All motives must be questioned, every claim
Assessed against those motives, every beast
Presumed a fox known by whatever name.

But shouldn't one be skeptical also
Of skepticism? After questioning
Beyond endurance, what do skeptics know?
Credulity may be the very thing
That saves those who without it would succumb
To mind-made beasts there's no escaping from.

Veiled Events

You did not think about it long. Why should
You have? The slip (two numerals transposed)
You blamed on being harried. When you closed
The window on your hand, the likelihood
That this was one of more odd things you would
Be doing seemed remote. And when you dozed
Off at the theatre, you, of course, supposed
It due to nothing, nothing that a good
Night's sleep would not relieve. It's only now
That missed connections, unremembered names
Define too large a part of living to
Ignore that veiled events begin to show
You what they meant: the dread beyond all blames,
The furtive darkness closing in on you.

DAVID BERMAN

A Song for Lazarus

My soul, where have you been these many days
My eyes were closed in dreamless sleep? I woke,
And all the sleepy town arose and spoke
Of wonder till the air was set ablaze
With flaming talk. And change. The skeptic prays
While the devout repeatedly invoke
Odd precedents. The ordinary folk
Would like to ask — I see it in their gaze —
What happened, but they fear to learn and so
Walk past me blindly. Not that there is much
To tell, and what there is, is negative;
No trumpet sounded; no light came aglow.
My soul returned, and I, unfit to touch,
Decayed, stood up, because my Friend said: Live.

Jo Painted

Josephine Hopper, the artist's wife and model

Caught naked in a hurtful light, my hands
forever clutching pockets of the air
I brace against, I am the one who stands
engulfed by windows, smoking, waiting where
anyone can see me. I am she
who sits alone in furnished rooms, the shade
pulled halfway down; and that one there is me,
cringing in the doorway as a blade
of sunlight edges close.   I can be seen
on quiet roads, hot pavements, moving trains.
You thought to paint me out, erase me, clean
the canvas of my spillage. You took pains
to wear me down, my skin becoming sheer;
you colored in my face with your own fear.

Conversion

(After Georges de la Tour)

A nocturne of shadow deepens to frame
the pensive Magdalen as she sits alone,
her glinting jewels darken to common stone,
her fine clothes weave a red brocade of shame.
She contemplates the image of the flame
in the mirror, a taller chaperone
to the candle's graceful plume of light, shown
twice, as if meant to enlighten and inflame.

Conversion by candlelight: Mary's hands
rest on a skull in her lap, its ochre stain
the color of regret — to watch her choose
between mirror and candle, the demands
of self and truth, evokes a kindred pain
in anyone who has a past to lose.

Invisible Son

My brother's room; his raincoat on the door,
his sketches everywhere — tall ships at sea
and pastel girls, a cat, a willow tree —
his tangled socks and sweaters on the floor.
The room is kept just as it was before
he died and gained perfection. Silently
my parents mourn, they have no eyes for me —
I think no one can see me anymore.
Diminished to a crying in the gloom,
how can I match my brother and survive
unheard, invisible? I am at most
another shadow in his shadowy room
and guilty, guilty, being still alive
and hungering to kill my brother's ghost.

Premonition

A sort of surfacing it seemed to be,
As of a fish into the light and air
That for an instant, as it's hanging there,
With a strangely steadfast certainty
Takes up the currents of another sphere
Before it drops again into its own,
Heavy as a triply skipping stone
That will at last forever disappear.
Five gulls, their calls, the crescent moon and sky
(The gray unearthly white against the blue),
The spirit sounding things of sea and shore
Conjoin to lure my untrained ear and eye
To the endlessness of my own death —
Then leave me stranded here to live some more.

JACK BUTLER

The Interstellar Tourist Shows His Slides

There is, on Earth, a most amazing thing
not seen in other systems anywhere.
Her axis tilts, so there are *seasons* there:
they call them *summer, winter, fall,* and *spring.*
It doesn't sound like much, and yet they sing
and sing those changes, and they offer prayer
as dying blooms and grasses offer rare
perfume — not in the thought that it might bring
rejuvenation, but as the purest praise.
The aspens on their pristine mountains blaze
a yellow we have yet to master, and then snow
collects at altitude, as if to show
the loveliness of silence. From which begin
toads, jonquils, jays, and creeks. And then, and then —

Moments

What causes it — the strange felicity
That surges through the nerves when least expected
As sudden thankfulness sweeps over me,
And somehow I feel cared for and protected?
Then, cares that fill an ordinary day
Diffuse within a sense of being blessed;
For no good cause, guilt vanishes away
And anxious premonitions are repressed.
Perhaps it's merely chemicals released
Into the intricacies of the brain;
Perhaps some psychological stress has ceased,
Or paused, before returning once again —
Or, maybe, other factors are bestowing
The moments that arrive to keep me going.

THOMAS CARPER

Why Did The

Because the cackling of the cocks and hens
Had raised his hackles for too many years.
Because the pecking order made no sense,
But simply fattened the inferiors.
Because the smells — not only of the yard,
But of the mental air — had made him sick,
With every hatchling hurrying to discard
The truths he had been raised on as a chick.
Because his spirit was oppressed by Freud,
The prince of darkness, and by Darwin's laws
That left the whole farm falling into void
No fowl could find a reason for. Because
The barnyard now seemed ready to explode,
With hope in flight, the chicken crossed the road.

THOMAS CARPER

Counting the Seconds

I always thought it was somewhat mystical
to have the lighthouse talking to us.
— R. v.d.H.

Sailing through the pounding swells at night,
The wind abeam tossing up sheets of spray,
We scan a black horizon for the light
That can assure us we are on our way
Toward home, a berth, a port on the solid shore
Far distant, though we sense we're drawing near,
Where, rounding a buoy, anchoring once more,
The landscapes so long loved will reappear.
When flashes finally penetrate the dark,
We time the intervals whose lengths declare
Which lighthouse speaks, and know we're on the mark,
Guided by steadfast signs of human care
That reach out calmly, over the swirling sea,
To send their message saying, "Follow me."

Roadside Crosses

This is a state where nothing marks the spot
officially. They crop up now and then
out on the Freeway, or in rustic plots
sometimes, near S-curves in the country, when
the corn's knee-high: a cross, or even two
or three, made out of poles or boards, white-
washed or painted. They seem to have a view
of nothing at all: only the blurred lights
of oncoming cars, and the eighteen-wheelers
roaring by.   Memory has a harsh sting —
blown back like the fine grit that settles
while you walk here now — no special healer,
merely a friend or brother stopped to bring
a can of flowers, to set among the nettles.

Summer Rain

We need a rain. It would be good to have
that motion sweeping out across the land —
that rhythm that rejuvenates, and leaves
unfurled, above the clouds, a lustrous band.
The meadow quickens under myriad drops,
the mill-race tumbles with the flow, and teams
of horses shelter on the bridge, or stop
beneath the oak, caught by the lightning's gleam.
We need that memory, that force. The blight
of things gone parched and sere has left a mark
upon our lives. When will we know again
that simple healing power? How many nights
must we lie sleepless in the gathering dark,
until we hear the wind, and then the rain?

Dark Matter

for J.G.

Out from the primal star that sprang unique
Before all others from the void: inflamed,
Inflationary, monstrous in its framed
And failing particles that into weak
And strong — electric — gravitational fields
Dispersed, and so began that headlong fall
Through time and space —
                         And was the brightness all
That ever was or came to be? One yield?
Or is there presence back before, beyond
That glowing pulse, that opens inwardly
Upon — into — some other realm? The way
Can only be imagined, like the bond
Of faith that points us to the mystery:
He is not here, but risen, on this day.

BRYCE CHRISTENSEN

English 101

for Bo

You died on Wednesday morning during an hour
I spent in telling 20 freshmen how
to put a comma next to *and* or *or*.
No nurse in ICU would ever know
the cousin who once dared to wade out deep,
out past the stumps, to catch the frog we kept
inside a coffee can, who scaled the steep
old treehouse roof, then coaxed me up. Who wept
when monitors went still? It should have been
the one who shared with you those summer days.
(How could we know they would not come again?)
Instead, RN's, well trained by their TA's,
filled out official forms to close your file,
deploying commas in the proper style.

The Sitter

(Vanessa Bell, Nude, *c. 1922-3, Tate Britain)*

Depressed and disagreeable and fat —
That's how she saw me. It was all she saw.
Around her, yes, I may have looked like that.
She hardly spoke. She thought I was a bore.
Beneath her gaze I couldn't help but slouch.
She made me feel ashamed. My face went red.
I'd rather have been posing on a couch
For some old rake who wanted me in bed.
Some people made me smile, they made me shine,
They made me beautiful. But they're all gone,
Those friends, the way they saw this face of mine,
And her contempt for me is what lives on.
Admired, well-bred, artistic Mrs. Bell,
I hope you're looking hideous in Hell.

Stress

(for Henry Thompson, but not about him)

He would refuse to put the refuse out.
The contents of the bin would start to smell.
How could she be content? That idle lout
Would drive the tamest woman to rebel.
And, now that she's a rebel, he frequents
The pub for frequent drink-ups with a mate
Who nods a lot whenever he presents
His present life at home as far from great.
The drinking makes his conduct even worse
And she conducts herself like some poor soul
In torment. She torments her friends with verse,
Her protest poems — dreadful, on the whole.
We daren't protest. Why risk an upset when
She's so upset already? I blame men.

Anima

One of those dismal, end-of-autumn nights
I came around a bend and saw her there,
standing beside the road as though my lights
had conjured her from dark, rain-ridden air.
Twenty years old at most, slender, frail,
she stood with shoulders hunched against the rain,
her black hair pulled back in a ponytail,
her face a mask of disbelief and pain.
Poor soul . . . I knew exactly who she was
and thought of stopping there to help her when
she vanished suddenly, no doubt because
she knew I doubted she had ever been
anything more than my imaginings
projected on a darkened world of things.

BILL COYLE

Time of Departure

To Lennart Karlsson

The mildest spell of weather since September —
A beach day, crowed the TV weathermen,
the warmest March anyone can remember —
ends, and it's dead of winter once again.
By three o'clock, the skies have turned so somber
(color of ashes, suitable for Lent)
we've lost our fledgling faith in spring and summer,
lost faith as well in all they might have meant.

Father, permit that we of little faith
may trust in things as basic as the seasons,
the busy sky above, the love of friends.
Ensure that this, that all our goings forth,
offer themselves as suitable occasions
to praise the Love on which this world depends.

Bookends

My mom prefers Sinatra to the Dead.
Where I wear denim, what she likes is silk.
Vacations she prefers are nature's sights
(not art museums): mountains or Nag's Head.
She drinks black coffee; mine is frothed with milk.
I never once inhaled, but she smoked "lites."
She, like my daughter, loves to watch tv,
and, luckily, they both take care of me.
My daughter, 25, commuting, whirls
into the city and back out, pursued
by sounds of retro music. She unfurls
her banner at a beach house; has reviewed
my mother's jewelry case and borrowed pearls.
They've both agreed to never get tattooed.

For Richard Wilbur

How many sit down with me when I write?
Frustrated lovers, manqué clergymen,
the lost who've little else to do with night
than wrap an angry fist around a pen,
those too-much hurt who scribble heartfelt lines
that, come the day, not even they can face?
What might have been! What almost was! reminds:
insight is not assured by falls from grace.

But then I think of one who drew on wit
and wakefulness to honor what he saw
with what none see, who took his civic gift
into the tigered wood to map our days
in fitting forms that keep the eye's first awe,
that order flux. And order us to praise.

Cineplex

They never go the way you think they should,
The movies showing at the cineplex:
There's too much violence, too much sex,
Too little modesty in Hollywood.
You can't believe the stories any longer,
Enjoy the *mise en scène,* or like the actors.
Violence that even its detractors
Are fascinated by, and ever stronger
And technically more enterprising effects
Have made the movies circuses of gore.
And yet, for all their sanguinary defects,
Cartoonish excesses, and tedium,
We go to them in droves, return for more,
Ignore the message, love the medium.

ROBERT DASELER

First Sight

You know how sometimes you'll look at a picture
Of a girl somewhere, taken years ago
And half a world away, seeming to show
Her happiness that instant in a flicker
Of mischief or delight, and you'll gaze
At her a minute, moved almost to tears,
Jolted by the recognition: Here's
One who might have cured my life's malaise.

Her image haunts the page, not beautiful,
Exactly, or the sort that other men
Would care for, but, now you've seen it, you'll
Remember her as if she'd kissed your cheek
Or walked the dawn-lit streets with you back then
And loved you for an hour or a week.

ROBERT DASELER

Men's Talk

She smiled on him that night but changed her mind
As he was talking, dismissing him with
A fatal yawn. Men of wit and pith
Advanced with her, but this one fell behind
By talking too much, working too hard
To win a favor all but achieved.
Afterward he sulked, taking it hard
And considering himself the more deceived.

The weakness of our sex is that we can't
Shut up. We almost always talk too much,
Trying to get what we concisely want
By yielding every secret that we own.
We want a word, perhaps a touch,
A promise that we won't be left alone.

At the Reception

From *"Small Talk"*

Oh look, there's What's-his-name . . . No, that's *my* drink . . .
And he's important these days, isn't he?
The *Times* gave him a good review, I think.
I'm sure he'd love to read my poetry.
You know him, don't you? Can't we go and mingle,
And you could introduce me as your friend?
I'll slip my ring off. There, I'm almost single.
This blouse works pretty well if I just bend
A little forward, no? That's sure to get him.
Well, go on then. Oh, who's that awful blonde?
He'd notice me if only she would let him . . .
I wish that I could wave a magic wand . . .
Hey look, she's gone. Come on . . . Why hi! He*llo*
I'm such a crazy fan of yours, you know.

DANA DELIBOVI

Snake Tattoo

A snake tattoo was coiled around her arm,
  hideous and black as she was pretty.
She exposed it with an unconscious charm,
  telling the whole bar she did it, "just to see."

Her serpent lay against the kind of skin
  uncommon, now that beauties like to tan,
a lovely column, propping up her chin,
  but vandalized from her elbow to her hand.

What would prompt such a girl to such a scar?
  to endure the blasphemy of the spike
injecting toxins into each soft pore?

The same reason people sat at the bar,
  eyeing her arm, betraying their dislike
of silent evenings on a houseless shore.

In Winter Light

As north wind makes the year's first snowflakes dance,
one of them drops into my hand like some
white Athens fallen into history's palm —
a moment's Parthenon, brief as a glance.

Rodin sculptured the world-enfolding Hand
which wrapped the empires as they waxed and waned,
enclosed the forms of Phidian snow, contained
the crystal heaven Plato's thought had spanned.

This snowflake on a visit from the skies
may be a flourishing metropolis
with teeming markets, proud Acropolis,
which I, a moment's god, hold as it dies.

If atoms dream in a space we cannot know,
what kingdoms claim my melting star of snow?

ALFRED DORN

By Shaded Lamplight

I have been reading in a lyre-back chair
my past's most wanted words. The sheet I hold
feels new to the fingers, but I am aware
the undated writing is three decades old.

I snowed her house with letters that I knew
would be unhurriedly opened, hurriedly read.
Although her own to me were short and few,
blind wish invented what she left unsaid.

Bound by a waking dream, I watch her write —
Merle Oberon eyes and color-of-midnight hair.
But my hand holds an empty sheet, stark white,
its only words the ones imagined there.
This is the mail no carrier ever brought,
the letter never written, never thought.

Native Meditation

At midnight in the sitting-room, lights off,
TV off, in the aroma of log-light
With a large dram crystalled, and more than enough
To last the darkness of a philosophic night,
I contemplate how timber turns to ash
In a wintry fire. An energetic flame,
Rising and dying, rising, domestic dash
Uttered in hearth-light, speaks of love and shame,
A lonely, lyric husbandry of thought
And poetry, the curse of scholarship,
Work's albatross, this bitter, native sip
That is a liquid and ancestral cry
From thermal waters made in the year dot —
This hearth-flame rises and it will not die.

DOUGLAS DUNN

Night Watch

Parsing this silence is listening to wood.
Sky and the moon's off-yellow golden highway
Sprinkle across sleepless, nocturnal Tay —
Firth, stars, accessories of solitude.
Familiar rooftops, treetops, closing in
On the window, no longer protect me.
Birch, box, wall, and the skyline reject me,
And the parish breaks as sweat on my skin
As I watch the pulsing of my Gatsby-light
On the Angus shore. How many tons of Tay
Pass silently as I say this, careless,
Waiting? Any minute now, and the night
Will start to lighten as ounces of day
Seep from the sea's exhausted genesis.

RHINA P. ESPAILLAT

Contingencies

As if it mattered: still, you probe to trace
precisely when it was fate took and tossed
and overwhelmed you, find the very place
it was you stood on when you found — or lost —
the thing that mattered. When the envelope
slid through the slot, innocent as a stone;
what you were scrubbing when you wiped the soap
hastily on your apron, took the phone
and left the water running, out of breath
with interruptions, slow to grasp the news:
the baby's birthweight, say, or time of death,
or diagnosis, casual as a fuse;
or in some public room, the stranger's name
half-heard, and nothing afterward the same.

Discovery

Lifting the phone to call, he heard her laugh
on an extension: something had been said,
but what? and who had said it?   He was half
tempted not to replace it in its bed
but hold it there by his astounded ear
to hear her laugh again in that old way
he had not heard since — when? — some distant year.
But also half afraid what she might say
into some other ear elsewhere. He dropped
the phone into its cradle, and the room
went loudly still, as if his life had stopped
like a stopped clock, as if it were a tomb
haunted by sounds he knew he used to know
but had forgotten missing long ago.

JANE FRIEDMAN

Lying in Bed

The little things that keep us up at night —
a drip drip coming from the kitchen sink;
the entrancing glow of the streets and soft moonlight;
the heater rattling on, clink by clink.
Two thrown-off sheets and sweat above my lip,
the windows open, breezes blowing in.
Both hands and fingers grasping the air, no grip,
but shadows touch the walls, acting the twin.
The curse of overactive minds I know,
for the art of sleeping well is lost on me,
when I remember your leaving years ago
and sleep away from where I thought I'd be.
Then you laugh someplace and mention my small name.
I wake to hear you; nothing is the same.

Driving in the Dark

Nightmare: I slowly approach an intersection
in the dark, try to turn on the headlights.
You tell me no, there is a county sanction
against it. Driving in the dark excites
the locals and we must conform, obey
the rules — "when in Rome" — and that invites
an argument. I say that I can't see;
it isn't safe. You have me increase the speed,
close my eyes, and, on the count of three,
run the intersection. I must concede
it works. Now, arc after black arc
of no-light flashes. We can read
the downhill roadsigns easily, each mark
in Braille: CAUTION SPEED UP RUSH THE DARK

CAROL FRITH

Walking Past Me

I see you walking through the airport, thin
and pale as if you were a child. I send
up words to follow you. Your shoulders bend
in that familiar way. You turn, and in
the place you were, there's no one. I feel my skin
remember you in fragments. I try to mend
the edges — language, touch — but in the end,
your memory collapses, and I begin
again: arrivals and departures on
the board — I lose myself in datelines. This
is called preparing. An orange exit light
is blinking down the hallway: you have gone,
turning through your slow unsteadiness,
walking past me till I'm out of sight.

The Road

He sometimes felt that he had missed his life
By being far too busy looking for it.
Searching the distance, he often turned to find
That he had passed some milestone unaware,
And someone else was walking next to him,
First friends, then lovers, now children and a wife.
They were good company — generous, kind,
But equally bewildered to be there.

He noticed then that no one chose the way —
All seemed to drift by some collective will.
The path grew easier with each passing day,
Since it was worn and mostly sloped downhill.
The road ahead seemed hazy in the gloom.
Where was it he had meant to go, and with whom?

D. R. GOODMAN

The Question of Suicides at Niagara Falls

Not why they go, but how we stay on shore,
One instant from the current's breathless pull,
Its power palpable, hypnotic, full
Of nature's swift relentlessness. And more:
How anyone can live for miles from here —
This undercurrent draining, like a dull,
Hard weight on every spirit, and the chill
Of ominous, grey rapids always near,
Forever sweeping downward, toward the roar
And plume of some calamity. The force
Of dizzying descent, the edge, compels:
One's mind, like any raft, swept to the core,
Must ride this glassy water on its course
Of rapid no return. We grip the rails.

R. S. GWYNN

Shakespearean Sonnet

With a first line taken from the TV listings

A man is haunted by his father's ghost.
A boy and girl love while their families fight.
A Scottish king is murdered by his host.
Two couples get lost on a summer night.
A hunchback slaughters all who block his way.
A ruler's rivals plot against his life.
A fat man and a prince make rebels pay.
A noble Moor has doubts about his wife.
An English king decides to conquer France.
A duke finds out his best friend is a she.
A forest sets the scene for this romance.
An old man and his daughters disagree.
A Roman leader makes a big mistake.
A sexy queen is bitten by a snake.

R. S. GWYNN

At Rose's Range

Old Gladys, in lime polyester slacks,
Might rate a laugh until she puts her weight
Squarely behind the snubnosed .38,
Draws down and pulls. The bulldog muzzle cracks
And barks six times, and six black daisies flower
Dead in the heart of Saddam's silhouette.
She turns aside, empties, reloads, gets set
And fires again. This goes on for an hour.

Later, we pass the time at the front door
Where she sits smoking, waiting for the friend
Who drives her places after dark: *You know,*
Earl's free next month. He says he wants some more
Of what she's got, and she's my daughter so
I reckon there's just one way this can end.

The Great Fear

Here where the door stands open, lights are on.
Each object occupies a special place.
Note the half sheet of foolscap by the phone
Where numbers someone labored to erase
Have left impressions. And there's no dial tone.
The tv glows, turned down. Dark figures chase
One who must learn no mercy can be shown
In such an extraordinary case.

An individual was here, but who?
His sheets are cold, the paperback romance
Gapes open, dog-eared, while his hanging pants
And belt await him. There is nothing missing,
Nor any sound except the kettle hissing,
Ready for the next one, whose name is You.

Groves of Academe

The hour dragged on, and I was badly needing
coffee; that encouraged my perversity.
I asked the students of Poetry Writing,
"Tell me about the poetry you're reading."
There was some hair chewing and some nail biting.
Snowdrifts piled up around the university.
"I've really gotten into science fiction."
"I don't read much — it breaks my concentration.
I wouldn't want to influence my style."
"We taped some Sound Poems for the college station."
"When *I* give readings, should I work on diction?"
"Is it true that no really worthwhile
contemporary poets write in rhyme?"
"Do you think it would be a waste of time
to send my poems to *Vanity Fair*?
I mean — could they relate to my work there?"

RACHEL HADAS

The Old Apartment

From "Dream Houses"

Given a dream house, once again I ride
north with incredible deliberation
up past 116th and Riverside.
Two fellow passengers talk to me in tandem
about their country and their destination.
Behind her face I peer, over his shoulder;
look out the window seemingly at random.
Greyness is growing, and it's getting colder.
Our glacial pace, though, clearly lets me see
the awning and the number and the stair.
Earl, the old doorman, would admonish me:
"Don't fall down, now!" as I went in and out.
Now people I don't know are living there,
their windows shining. We inch out of sight.

RACHEL HADAS

The Dead Poet

From "Dream Houses"

Given a dream house, I know how I feel.
A year and more of honoring the dead
and a partition opens to reveal
two rooms where I had thought was only one.
Yet neither had a desk or chair or bed.
How, if he lived here, did he sleep or write?
In this authorial mausoleum
no worktable exists, no day, no night.
Less mausoleum, though, than cenotaph:
what pilgrims tramp through is a neutered place,
bare of his presence (that cocked head, that laugh)
and barer still of why they came to see
the residue of years in such a space,
empty of what he left us: poetry.

SUSAN HAMLYN

Interflora

From Robert B. @ mailexcite dot com
To E.B.B. @ virgin dot uk:
Please find herewith a proof of my esteem
a customized, fresh, virtual bouquet.
For scent please click on cellophane and press
Control. To read the message on the tag
highlight the print, click on *Encrypt Reverse.*
To unwrap blooms and place in vase use *Drag.*
My flowers sent, beloved, in this way,
won't fade, stink of mortality's decay.
Petals won't wilt to husks nor leaves to slime;
these on-line flowers for you will outlast Time.
But if, my love, this gift seems incomplete
and does not touch your heart, then press *Delete.*

GWEN HARWOOD

A Game of Chess

To John Brodie

Nightfall: the town's chromatic nocturne wakes
dark brilliance on the river; colours drift
and tremble as enormous shadows lift
Orion to his place. The heart remakes
that peace torn in the blaze of day. Inside
your room are music, warmth and wine, the board
with chessmen set for play. The harpsichord
begins a fugue; delight is multiplied.

A game: the heart's impossible ideal —
to choose among a host of paths, and know
that if the kingdom crumbles one can yield
and have the choice again. Abstract and real
joined in their trance of thought, two players show
the calm of gods above a troubled field.

An Acrostic Birthday Greeting

To A. D. Hope

Alec, to whom my debt is quite unpayable,
Hear me before great ruining time has dimmed
All of my wits and made these words unsayable:
Peerless you are and shall be, rightly hymned,
Parnassian, in the laurelled crown you wear.
Your birthday's one of import to the nation.
Bear me, loved Muse, to Canberra, to share
If only in a dream your celebration.
Remember me, far off, in spirit near,
Taking my glass and blowing you a kiss.
Haec olim meminisse . . . Cradled in
Delight, I trust, you drink in utter bliss
Among old friends and lovers, to begin
Your best-to-be, your eighty-seventh year.

SEAMUS HEANEY

The Skylight

from "Glanmore Revisited"

You were the one for skylights. I opposed
Cutting into the seasoned tongue-and-groove
Of pitch pine. I liked it low and closed,
Its claustrophobic, nest-up-in-the-roof
Effect. I liked the snuff-dry feeling,
The perfect, trunk-lid fit of the old ceiling.
Under there, it was all hutch and hatch.
The blue slates kept the heat like midnight thatch.

But when the slates came off, extravagant
Sky entered and held surprise wide open.
For days I felt like an inhabitant
Of that house where the man sick of the palsy
Was lowered through the roof, had his sins forgiven,
Was healed, took up his bed and walked away.

ANTHONY HECHT

The Witch of Endor

I had the gift, and arrived at the technique
That called up spirits from the vasty deep
To traffic with our tumid flesh, to speak
Of the unknown regions where the buried keep
Their counsel, but for such talents I was banned
By Saul himself from sortilege and spell
Who banished thaumaturges from the land
Where in their ignorance the living dwell.

But then he needed me; he was sore afraid,
And begged for forbidden commerce with the dead.
Samuel he sought, and I raised up that shade,
Laggard, resentful, with shawl-enfolded head,
Who spoke a terrible otherwordly curse
In a hollow, deep, engastrimythic voice.

AMY HELFRICH

A Young Girl's Solace

She hears the distant motion of the train;
its tattered singing in the hollow night
sweeps across the worn and tired plain
that sleeps beneath a winter's quilt of white.
Rumbling slowly past, the headlight streams
into the dusty corners of her room,
hypnotizing shadows with its beams
while warding off the angry midnight gloom.
And as the light patrols, she lies awake
and waits, the covers clutched up to her ears,
until the whistle signals she can take
her eyes away from all the unseen fears.
For in the ragged engine's grunts and sighs,
she gathers all its pulsing lullabies.

AMY HELFRICH

The Drought

At dusk, he moves among the dying plains
of winter wheat and walks a sharpened pace
to stretch the life that's puddled in his veins,
muster up some color in his face,
and see what he can salvage from the dust:
this season's bitterness has starved his grain
and left the soil with nothing but a trust
that time will make a friend out of the rain.
So now he wanders through the field he's turned
and tilled with care, a twenty acre grave
it seems. And, yet, because in years he's learned
that, often times, there's something left to save,
he stops to sift the dusty earth in hands
that look for breath inside the broken lands.

The Guard

His words clutched like a drowning man's embrace
Those nights he spilled his secrets on my porch.
I helped him sort them, find each fear a place
Within the sanctuary of his church,
Others' opinions. Crying at times, he swore
I was the only person he could trust.
I reassured him that his private war
Was safe between us, and that problems must
Deliver change. On that score I was right:
By winter he'd stopped calling, and I heard
Through mutual friends that he took great delight
In quoting me for laughs. And yet I guard
His secrets, rocking on my porch alone,
Each hour imagining I hear the phone.

Hard Bop

I need to get some rhythm in my speech,
a soulful sort of sultry syncopation;
notes too high, too low, to easily reach,
a riff to proclaim my conflagration.
A drumbeat pounds, a backbeat of desire
that sounds across my Serengeti Plain,
enchanted dance around a swirling fire,
singeing love is singing through my veins.
Hot licks and crazed improvisation styles,
the whispered tune of limbs and lips and sighs,
as sweet as any solo played by Miles,
as shocking as my first glimpse of your eyes.
If only I could play a be-bop tune
that burns the burn I burn when I'm with you.

MARK JARMAN

She is a cloud in her own sunny day . . .

(Unholy Sonnets, #15)

She is a cloud in her own sunny day,
The damp spot on a rock under the lip.
She is the flaw that cracks the fired clay,
The bubble that will break the binding slip.
She is the world after the rapture comes,
The one left in the field, the one left grinding.
History over, she's the drop that drums
In drainpipes without anybody minding.
She is the definition of alone.
And I am one who makes things up about her,
The way the sky makes weather for the earth.
And she is one who lets that happen to her,
The way the dirt will let you take a stone
Into your hand and calculate its worth.

MARK JARMAN

Breath like a house fly batters the shut mouth . . .

(Unholy Sonnets, #24)

Breath like a house fly batters the shut mouth.
The dream begins, turns over, and goes flat.
The virus cleans the attic and heads south.
Somebody asks, " What did you mean by that?"
But nobody says, "Nothing," in response.
Silence becomes the question and the answer.
The ghost abandons all of his old haunts.
The body turns a last cell into cancer.
And then — banal epiphany — and then,
Time kick starts and the deaf brain hears a voice.
The eyes like orphans find the world again.
Day washes down the city streets with noise.
And oxygen repaints the blood bright red.
How good it is to come back from the dead!

Candle

One star has faded from our evening sky.
Millions remain; its loss is meaningless,
but on some world in bitter emptiness
of space, what terrors did its death imply?
What navigators watched their pole star die,
what shrines, whose majesty was somehow less,
burned incense to their gods and goddesses,
their avatar oblivious to their cry?

Although this happened long eons ago,
in reaches far beyond our present sight,
it may yet be important that we know,
for at this edge, that vanished stellar light,
that darkness where its fossil remnants glow,
reminds us we are on the rim of night.

The Plot

(after Borges' "The Plot")

Destiny loves repetition, symmetries:
Caesar, attacked by friends, is pressed to the base
of a statue by their knives. "Et tu, Bruté!",
he calls in anguish. Among his enemies
he sees the impassive and familiar face
of Marcus Junius Brutus, his protégé.

"You too, my son," will echo in the themes
of poem and drama like a recurring dream.

Centuries pass. Somewhere in the Argentine,
some gauchos attack their leader. He falls, betrayed.
His adopted son is among them. In his pain,
he calls out to him. Through the flashing blades,
he cannot see Destiny smile from the mezzanine,
or know he is slain so a scene may be replayed.

ELIZABETH JENNINGS

Having It Both Ways

What liberty we have when out of love,
Our heart's back in its place, our nerves unstrung,
Time cannot tease us, and once more we move
In step with it. Out of love we're strong,

Without its yearnings and the way it makes
All virtues vices. Steady liberty
Is our element and no heartbreaks
Can touch or take us. We are nobly free.

But how long can we live within this state?
Don't we miss the slow encroachment of
Possessive passion? Don't we half-await

Its cruel enchantments which no longer have
Power over us? O we are obdurate,
Begging for freedom, hankering for love.

The Way They Live Now

You make love and you live together now
Where we were shy and made love by degrees.
By kiss and invitation we learnt how
Our love was growing. You know few of these

Tokens and little gifts, the gaze of eye
To eye, the hand shared with another hand.
You know of few frustrations, seldom cry
With passion's stress, yet do you understand

The little gestures that would mean so much,
The surging hope to be asked to a dance?
You take the whole of love. We lived by touch

And doubt and by the purposes of chance
And yet I think our slow ways carried much
That you have missed — the guess, the wish, the glance.

CARRIE JERRELL

The Ring

It's overwhelming for the unprepared:
checking for flaws with magnifying loupes,
the color grades, the setting choices, the flared
four-prong cathedral, contour ridges, with flutes
of baguette accents down the sides. The bands,
once standard 14k gold, now come
in aircraft-grade titanium. It stands
to reason, one would think, as rings become
unbreakable the bonds they represent
might, too. But every master jeweler knows
about the unseen structural punishment
the gems undergo — the blades, the saws, the blows
received at every facet, the grinding hours
it takes for shapes like "teardrops," "hearts," and "flowers."

CARRIE JERRELL

The Processional

("Here Comes the Bride")

It comes from Wagner's opera *Lohengrin,*
when Elsa weds the knight whose identity
she swore she'd never ask. But mystery
is always overwhelming — the heroine
betrays their love to learn his name, and when
he disappears across the river, she
calls after him, then dies in agony.

The congregation rises. The strings begin
to play. Out steps another Elsa, veiled
today from the truth that all love coexists
with death. She's now a momentary queen,
starting her own long walk from fairy tale
first-act to tragic final scene, who risks
them both for all the drama in between.

Interruptions

I like it when my poems wake me up
and rouse me from my bed to force my hand
to seize a pen and scribble fleeing thoughts
before they fade away and disappear,
becoming words that no one ever hears
because I let them drift away. You ought
to rise to try it too. When poems land
smack-dab into your life, you have to stop
and bring them to this world, so strong and clear
they'll stun us all, so right and finely wrought.
Good poems have this knack, they interrupt
whatever else is going on, so taut
with apt wisdom, so just in their demand —
they're like the finest kind of reprimand.

ALLISON JOSEPH

Miss Organization

My life's controlled by swelling paper piles:
rough drafts go here, and syllabi right there,
that one's for worthy causes I should care
about, this one's for frequent flyer miles
and credit card reports, the run of bills
that tell me what my spending limits are.
The journey to insolvency's not far,
so should I save or spend it all on thrills?
I'll tell you what my greatest thrill would be —
to live without these piles, all orderly —
or maybe just a neater symmetry —
no more receipts gone loose, my desktop free,
no more piles on the floor or in my bed.
Don't even ask what piles dwell in my head.

Note from Echo

Narcissus, I no longer haunt the canyons
and the crypts. I thrive and multiply;
uncounted daughters are my new companions.

We are the voicemail's ponderous reply
to the computers making random calls.
We are the Muzak in the empty malls,
the laughtrack on the reruns late at night,
the distant siren's chilling lullaby,
the steady chirp of things that simplify
their scheduled lives. You know I could recite
more, but you never cared for my recitals.

I do not miss you, do not need you here —
I can repeat the words of your disciples
telling lovers what they want to hear.

Cancer Prayer

Dear Lord,
             Please flood her nerves with sedatives
and keep her strong enough to crack a smile
so disbelieving friends and relatives
can temporarily sustain denial.

Please smite that intern in oncology
who craves approval from department heads.

Please ease her urge to vomit; let there be
kind but flirtatious men in nearby beds.

Given her hair, consider amnesty
for sins of vanity; make mirrors vanish.

Surround her with forgiving family
and nurses not too numb to cry. Please banish
trite consolations; take her in one swift
and gentle motion as your final gift.

A.M. JUSTER

The Night Pro Wrestling Was Real

The new recruit was named "The Silent Sheik"
Although he lacked a trace of Arab blood
And droned all week about his honed physique.

The script had called for "The Stupendous Stud"
To climb out of his litter, preen and flaunt
Then take the mike to make a sneering taunt,
But Sheik reached out and grabbed Stud's pompadour
Then slammed him down with a resounding thud.
Security was greeted with a flood
Of jeers and crumpled programs, but before
The end real blood ran faster than free beer.

Distress about this mess was genuine.
The hero lost, the moral was not clear,
And most true fans believed the fix was in.

HOLLY KARAPETKOVA

Parts of Speech

Tomorrow, I will build a universe
of ink, and write you subject to my pen,
controlling all you do and think in verse
and changing every loss of mine to win;
for instance, I could start with adjectives,
crossing out the *old* that I've become,
replacing *dull* with *lovely;* or I'd give
your *careless* words a turn to *grateful* ones.
And then for nouns — inscribe your *apathy*
as *care* with but a movement of my wrist,
to trade *distaste* for *passion,* transform *me*
into *she,* and thus by you as her be kissed.
Or better than this wordy love-retrieving,
I'll simply stop all verbs, keep you from leaving.

Harriet

Bullied by Pound, ran "Prufrock" in the back
Of a dull summer number — shot heard round
The world. Rattling across Siberia
By railcar over tundra, stony ground
Where stunted fir trees struggled to breathe free
Like poets in America, she'd found
Her vision. Stuck out chin — by God, she'd pack
Not pork but poetry.

Vestal, bluestockinged battler — what hard nights
She spent uprooting tick-tock lyricists,
Sowing and weeding fields of neophytes.
Who could have thought the Mountain of the Mists
Would keep her grave when, frail, on Andes heights,
She closed eyes that had blazed like amethysts?

X. J. KENNEDY

Others

The lurker in his jack-o'-lantern mask
   Soliciting small boys to sell him feels,
   Transvestites wobbling by on quaking heels,
The red-eyed bums who haunt dark parks to ask
Lone passersby of either sex for sex,
   Women who put their bodies up for bids
   Or, to retain their lovers, drown their kids,
The shooter-up who shotgun-slays his ex
For seeing other men — the record drips
   Carnage. Watching the nightly news scroll by,
   We say, There but for the grace of God go I,
As though their lives were our vicarious trips,
   But where we walk they loiter on the sly
And sometimes when we kiss we taste their lips.

Held

The raking done, the cut grass bagged and set
Upon the curb, he looks to clear a space
To rest where aching back and deck chair meet.
The twilight settles down at summer's pace
And draws his eye where western sky and sun
Conspire to paint his working day an end
Of gaudy purple fire. And though retired,
He feels the heft of tools still in his hand.
He holds his drink as if it were a haft
Of ash, and thinks of what that hand has done.
The frosted glass of lemonade, perspired
As dusk comes on, has one sweet swallow left.
He lifts it, like a chalice, in a toast
To night and all the toil he misses most.

Jogging the Bona Dea Trail

Whether or not we take the longest trail,
Called Serendipity, or simply take
The path to Walden Pond (a man-made lake),
A large map had drawn everything to scale
At the park's entrance: any way we choose —
From paths called Rabbit Run and Prairie Way
To the Swinging Bridge — offers familiar views,
Of pond and field, though what I mean to say
Is that despite the wooden ironies
Of verse I post along the way like signs,
Each foreknown pleasure of my life with you
Is like our jogging: Crossing the Dark Slough,
We leave behind the Black Swamp's stricken trees
And walk to light through miles of scented pines.

BRAD LEITHAUSER

After the Detonation of the Moon

Hate Winter? Here's a Scientist's
Answer: Blow Up the Moon
Headline, Wall Street Journal

We *were* overwhelmed, just as they'd intended:
for wasn't this the greatest show of clout
the world had ever seen, and all without
loss of a single life — an exploit splendid
no less for its humanity than for
its sweeping expertise? And they were right
that life would go on as it had. The night
was still the night. The stars blazed all the more
in a cleared sky.
                  These days we seldom fall
for that trick of the eye by which some tall
mist-softened clocktower or fogged street lamp will
recall a changing face, and something tidal
heave in the chest, then ebb, leaving us all
to wonder when if ever this sea too might still.

BRAD LEITHAUSER

From R.E.M.

What made the moment was the lack of all
Premeditation, calculation, talk:
Oh, I was *talking* (what, I can't recall)
Until, look catching look, we slowed our walk,
Stopped still. Right then, now, never having done
Anything on earth like this before, I brought
My face toward yours . . . You had no time for thought.
Instinct alone lifted your mouth to mine.

(The beauty was just this: there was no thinking.
And that I came undone at a mere kiss —
My mind a flood-rush like no flood's before,
Such that no past gasped groping, no headlong sinking
Of flesh in flesh could touch the force of this —
Was a boon, to be sure, but nothing more.)

I Conclude a Sonnet Never Changed

I conclude a sonnet never changed
a mind, or moved a heart, or opened a locked
door. If such could be so readily arranged,
poems could not possibly stay stocked.
Pockets would be filled and pillows swarmed.
Oh no, a sonnet never swung a gate,
cracked a safe, or left a bomb disarmed.
It never swam a moat, or pried a crate.
Or rather, whom it moved, at any rate,
was accidental; a side effect, some poor
someone tugged at when its influence, its weight,
its pool of moonlight revealed a midnight shore.
Yes, then, it may have changed a life, or more;
but not the one it was *intended* for.

The First to Know

I do not claim that it is always so,
but in this case, it would be fair to say:
the woman was the first to know.
It was the kind of truth that burrowed deep
inside of one and did not go away —
tenacious thing that rose up after sleep
to heal what bruised it in the heat of day.
Now, if there is a first, there follows then
there has to be a last, which would be he —
who takes the path of, well, so many men;
and so he fails to hear, and fails to see,
while they are playing games of touch and go . . .
it's she, you foolish man, it's she, it's she;
till finally . . . yes, but it was always so . . .

ANDREW LITTAUER

Drought

Two days ago I drove amid parched fields —
The alfalfa yellowing at the tip —
As the month-long drought refused to yield
Its day-in-day-out unrelenting grip.
I passed a farm where the reek of fresh manure
Sweetened by the scent of tasseling maize
For a brief moment helped my mind endure
The sight of pastures cropped to a brown baize.
These summer dog-days have cast their arid curse
That drains the streams until the gray stones cry
In aching silence, and water — life's wet-nurse —
Deserts the land as springs go slowly dry.
The ground grows hard, and dervishes of dust
Taunt us: tenants living on earth's fragile crust.

WILLIAM LOGAN

After a Line by F. Scott Fitzgerald

From "Long Island Sins"

Southampton, Hot Springs, and Tuxedo Park:
lost in the backwash of the Crash, the War,
the refugees of grace were washed ashore.
The girls who once were "miffed" or "truly vexed"
would soon acquire the morals of a shark,
waltzing the railroad barons round the floor,
their cold, triumphant necks a jewelry store.
And in the shadows the next drink, and the next.
Where does it go, the moment of desire?
Lost, rattling down the Special's corridor,
the distant vein of lights in semaphore;
lost, the champagne glasses tossed against the fire,
the bullet laid inside a lower drawer.
And there is love, cruel love, the last to bore.

ANTHONY LOMBARDY

Slumber Party

One hardly sees their faces. At thirteen
The girls dodge in with their half-hidden stashes
Of candy and secrets that cannot be seen
At all beneath their childlike, long eyelashes.
They nest like lab rats in a wealth of litter
Beneath the television where they grin
At all the foolish world that's old and bitter,
Prone to dying, and so inept at sin.

Untouched, they reach out from their girlish height
To the full possession of truths we only borrow.
May the saint of slumber parties guard their light
Till all of them are sleeping, that fear and sorrow
Again find somewhere else to spend the night
And someone else to wake up with tomorrow.

Casinos

Sweetness is the secret of casinos,
and fairness of a democratic kind.
If you're confused or lonely there, you'll find
a girl to show you everything she knows.
The dealers do not judge you and are blind
to shipwrecks of the ego and romance.
If you're not winning, credit circumstance,
and if you're up a little, who will mind?
Perhaps you'll square the circle at roulette,
and shame those dullards, industry and thrift,
(though Archytas is seeking that rule yet.)
The dice are easy things for you to toss
through nights that give to virtue such short shrift
and ready you for other forms of loss.

ANTHONY LOMBARDY

List

She's made her life a list of things to do.
Her friends become her clients, her clients friends,
because she plans things out and follows through
with calls and little gifts that show she cares.
(It's little things that make girls millionaires.)
It's something small that brings her down, as well,
that trips her when the scripted conference ends
in the humming, modular space of some motel,
where all the domestic comforts are in place.
But in such neutral darkness one is scared,
and suddenly the carpet burns the face,
something trips her that must not quite exist,
that in the quiet found her unprepared
and happened though it was not on her list.

Margin

The faintest scrawl along the margin, slight
Blue rendering of soul, the curlicue
Of passing years. I turn my reading light
To better catch the curves, the dots, the you
Inside my book. How hurriedly you penned
Those lines, the single page like yellow skin.
But, then, perhaps you saw it new, the blend
Of whitened pulp, the spine just breaking in,
The dog-ears yet to be. And did you dream
Of nights like this, before your soul's ascent
Above the earth, and know your words would seem
A mystery to my mind? Was your intent
To leave me here, trapped in another age,
Your world a fading scribble on my page?

SAMUEL MAIO

Had I Had Had Shakespeare as a Student

His freshperson year for "Composition,"
I would have closed both his plagiarist's eyes,
Averted his mind from those histories —
They're elitist, to be buried and done!
And as for Italian romance, cos, shun
It as sexist, vengeful, and cruel, those sighs
And all that plotting for some maiden's thighs.
Direct your spirit, I'd have said, to pen
Less comedy—for life's too serious
To treat lightly. And as for tragedy,
It's moribund, so male macho, and wrong!
I enlighten you, I in correctness
Free you of lies, slime, and patriarchy!
And never, ever, rhyme — that's for rap songs!

AMIT MAJMUDAR

Perspective

So what if art historians hold it dear?
I do not think perspective an advance,
Painting what portion of a room is near,
What farther off, so that the whole's enhanced.
I would prefer to look upon the world
With flat medieval eyes and never see
How far across the room she stands, this girl
Whom I would give up art itself to meet.
I do not have the hand to paint the pair
Of us together, nor the self-assured
Touch that would draw her chiaroscuro where
My shape could flush be overlaid on hers.
   Awaiting this revival in the art,
   I dream a movement that I cannot start.

AMIT MAJMUDAR

The Disruption

I had a world apart before we loved,
two poles, a compass, and a steady North,
a ground beneath me and a sky above,
no inland dark, no Indies to explore.
I had a universe before we met,
a routine sun, fixed stars, a clockwork moon.
My planets ran the orbits I had set
and played the old Pythagorean tune.
But now *you,* comet, chaos, love: rogue missile
of heatseeking fire, bullet astray
among celestial bodies: I fear your kiss will
break my strict night with your naked day
   and from my world's ribs rip a moon and rings
    as your strange tongue teaches my throat to sing.

A Query

I wonder how you're living with those things
I left — shirts I shed and gave to you,
that Mexican vase, poems I thought were true —
the hopeful clutter that a romance brings.
I wonder when you hear familiar songs,
the soundtrack that we made from old cassettes,
if music conjures what the days forget
or summons back a symphony of wrongs.
I wonder if you're walking down those streets
we walked together: do they look the same?
Now that we know that no one was to blame
and fate knew better, can memory turn sweet
the sour taste of two souls wrenching free
of things they hoped for which could never be?

CHARLES MARTIN

Even as We Sleep

Avoidance has found someone else to blame,
Obsession seeks a mantra to repeat,
And swift with *Panic*, runs across the street
In order not to have to deal with *Shame*,
Who urges *Rage* and *Folly* to come meet
Denial, going by another name;
Now unmarked cards cost *Honesty* the game,
As *Confidence* turns out to be *Deceit,*

And *Guilt* refuses to complain about
The way she's being treated by her men,
While ever-diffident *Anxiety*
Is wondering if best is not to be,
In this dark cavern between now and when,
Of whose existence he is much in doubt.

CHARLES MARTIN

Necessity's Children

"Necessity is the mother of invention."
— Old Saw

The other children of Necessity
Are utterly disheartened now, bereft
Of hopefulness since sweet Invention left,
Bravest and brightest of their family,
Who seemed to have no choice except to be
Original, persistent, shrewd, and deft;
For whom clear water sprang from the rock, cleft
By charms bespeaking her cool mastery.

"Ah, well," the others say, "she will be back,"
And armed with their conviction — for they know
How unremittingly impassable
The world, confronted by what they all lack,
Must seem to her — they say, "It will prove so:
Necessity is the mother of us all."

KATHERINE McALPINE

Island in Winter

Telephone poles, snapped by last night's gale,
litter the causeway, severing our link
to the mainland. The electric fixtures blink,
gasp, struggle for power, finally fail.
Snow, still falling, clogs the unplowed street.
"Stay home," exhorts the portable radio.
There are places I need and want to go,
serious obligations I must meet.
But weather wins, compelling me to stay
under the comforter with books and tea,
island within an island. Out at sea,
the foghorn's deep, muted, persistent bray
sings counterpoint to the shrill wind's lament.
I've never felt so safe or so content.

Note from Home

Should they read *Romeo and Juliet*
in freshman high-school English — just the time
when their hormonal systems start to get
wacky without any extra help and I'm
expecting, as it is, that poltergeists
will move in any minute? Here's my son,
for instance, helplessly over-heels with one
Jennifer, and contriving lunchroom trysts.
He has this stunned expression in his eyes,
stumbles about and heaves enormous sighs.
As you'll recall, being fourteen is hard
enough without encouraging the Bard
to fuel the fantasies that fill his head.
Maybe the kids could read *Macbeth* instead?

Solid Space

The dancers, blind electrons, twirl apart
And flicker quickly in and out of place,
So each one's course, impossible to chart,
Seems lost in empty, subatomic space.

Some law against attraction too intense
Compels resistance, unless something snaps.
It holds the pattern taut and so prevents
A final gravitational collapse.

We, too, my dear; each one of us seems fated
To be not really sure of where we are,
Our deepest hurts and longings orchestrated
To keep us not too close and not too far.

The subtle, strong connections are unseen —
What binds us is the distance in between.

SUSAN McLEAN

Cassandra

Because I turned him down, the god Apollo
cursed me with sight. The gift of art is not
the kind you can refuse. No matter what
you do or fail to do, the scenes will follow
you everywhere, assault you in your dreams.
Even if you could turn yourself to wood,
he'd force your hardened fingertips to bud,
and make a garland of your silent screams.
You don't believe me? Though I've heard you sneer
and call me crazy, still you'd have me offer
forecasts of the future. Apropos
of your young daughter, would you like to hear
what day she'll die and everything she'll suffer?
I thought not. No one really wants to know.

PETER MEINKE

Home on Cape Cod

We've seen colossal sights together, dazzling
to the heart: the rusty ruins of Petra
eroding in the Dead Sea winds, dark alleys
twisted through Luxor, the Nile, the Rhinefalls, Etna
in its bright burning, the brutal calendar
of Stonehenge, the Great Wall where we cried
out loud, overwhelmed by fright or wonder:
and the Gorge where Timothy slipped and nearly died.

Still, of all those visions that enthralled my eyes,
the one repeating daily like a muezzin's call,
is that of you, by our window in a dressing gown,
brushing your matchless hair, and saying with a sigh,
perhaps I *had* made you happy, after all:
I, and the little roses of Provincetown.

Mystery

. . . So there's the fire escape. And too many keys.
Beside the bed the empty glass accuses
no one, everyone. The Matron's eyes protrude
like gooseberries, her glance startled when she sees
the Inspector staring at her knees.
A page is missing from the book the Student
loaned the crippled Nurse, and beneath the huge
live oak the Butler scrabbles in the leaves.

Now, gathered in the library, the crime
gaping before us like a hungry hearse,
we clear our throat, we smooth our suit and dress.
Now the Inspector rises for the last time,
now the Matron the Student the Butler the Nurse,
we stiffen like corpses, crazy to confess . . . .

Card Party

for Alex

Now pause, as mothers everywhere do pause,
one hand to curtain, knob, or nursery door,
to listen for the breath that lifts before
the silence of the heart stopped without cause.
Anyone may chide us: we turn and laugh.
Of course the baby's fine, we say, and sip
our wine, poke the fire, paint a redder lip,
refill the nut dish, play a heart, or pass.

And yet, the househeart beats elsewhere, above
the merriment, the card-bright air, the din.
We slip away to listen, certain of
a pillow slipped, a choking toy — our sin —
and, bent like tardy angels overhead,
we breathe again with him to heal our dread.

TIMOTHY MURPHY

The Track of a Storm

Bastille Day, 1995

We grieve for the twelve trees we lost last night,
pillars of our community, old friends
and confidants dismembered in our sight,
stripped of their crowns by the unruly winds.
There were no baskets to receive their heads,
no women knitting by the guillotines,
only two sleepers rousted from their beds
by fusillades of hailstones on the screens.
Her nest shattered, her battered hatchlings drowned,
a stunned and silent junko watches me
chainsawing limbs from corpses of the downed,
clearing the understory of debris
while supple saplings which survived the blast
lay claim to light and liberty at last.

The Retarded Boys at the Gym

They sound like other boys their age, at first,
But any play of wit is accidental.
Their antics are by rote, though unrehearsed,
Their speech, the indecorum of the gentle.
Their bodies, too, seem heavier than ours.
Attendants must remind them to get dressed.
So evenhanded are the higher powers,
The boys are rarely scolded; never blessed.
The slowest tucks his shirt into his pants
And suddenly a spasm makes him twitch.
A quavering song accompanies his dance —
Some prankish demon's hand flicking a switch.
He buttons all his buttons as he should.
And God looks on his work and finds it good.

The Opera

Callas. La Scala. *Tosca.* '53.
Strange, I remember only I was there.
Now the recordings haunt me: poignancy
Of "Vissi d'arte" can lacerate the air
When listening by myself. You were beside me
That evening in Milan. Were just *beside*?
No happier preposition? — Donne could guide me —
When touches, alert and thermal, first confide?

Recall that emperor, "Stupor Mundi"? — meaning
The World's Amazement. Meaning stupor too.
Glory can blind, as once it did by screening
Sets, theater, and diva. Close to you
Learning, I dazzled in the sidewise light
Till love's halation became second sight.

JOHN FREDERICK NIMS

Strange!

I'd have you known! It puzzles me forever
To hear, day in, day out, the words men use,
But never a single word about you, never.
Strange! — in your every gesture, worlds of news.
On busses people talk. On curbs I hear them;
In parks I listen, barbershop and bar.
In banks they murmur, and I sidle near them;
But none allude to you there. None so far.

I read books too, and turn the pages, spying:
You must be there, one beautiful as you!
But never, not by name. No planes are flying
Your name in lacy trailers past the blue
Marquees of heaven. No trumpets cry your fame.

Strange! — how no constellations spell your name!

JESSICA PIAZZA

On Edward Hopper's "New York Movie"

Is it depression or her senseless shoes,
that lean the usher's frame against the wall
and shut her eyes before the languid sprawl
of limbs upon the cushioned seats? Bemused
with some young sorrow or lamenting those
black velvet straps that cut such burning rifts
along her failing, pretty feet? She lifts
her careful fingers to her chin. She chose
those lovely sandals to defy the tough,
misshapen fabric of her uniform.
Her shapely wrists peek out beneath the cuff,
her ivory cheeks are crimson-stained and warm.
The woman bows her head in the muted light,
as starlets laugh in perfect black and white.

Four Winter Flies

Lost and stumbling across the window,
They want the light that looks like warmth until
I lift the sash and off they go,
Blown in a brief cold gust that stuns, its chill

Leaving them slow to recover. Then they return,
Dotting the glass, tracing what they cannot touch
Until they're vacuumed up and out to turn
Into the earth for which they've swarmed so much.

May each buzz back behind its thousand eyes
To pace the unforgiving pane where sight
Said "come" and it could not and died,
As all die, opposite the world's long light

Whose bare-limbed seepage and shallowing rise
Once proved the brief ellipsis of four late flies.

CHARLES RAFFERTY

City Skies

This close to Philadelphia the stars
get blotted out by billboard lights, the blaze
of office buildings mixed with haze, the cars
that keep on coming. There's little to praise
about a sky like this, which we bemoan
for its simplicity. It holds nothing
like the complicated gauze of our own
galaxy. For this, we feel there's something
somehow missing. If any lights appear
they are descending jets, the gaudy beams
above a dealership. They make it clear
we crouch beside a city, but what redeems
us is the moon, rising like a prayer,
there above the bank, the siren-filled air.

Mazeway

I have this diagram inside my brain
that helps me navigate the world outside,
to find those trails that others try to hide,
to search out secret tracks without a strain
then orient myself in strange terrain,
and stroll dark passageways without a guide.
This chart has always left me satisfied
that I am never wandering in vain.

But lately I've begun to doubt this map.
Perhaps it's time to rearrange the lines,
erase those boundaries which overlap,
reshaping any border which confines,
escaping all the mazes which entrap,
thus freeing up my mind for new designs.

Sixteen

After eight straight weeks of summer drought,
the tomatoes hang deflated in the yard;
even the weeds have flickered and gone out.
I water anyway, the lonely guard
of hard dry rows of beans, a burning lawn.
Inside, my daughter slinks — a perfumed sigh
and too-tight shorts. She shouts she's off, is gone
in a flash and a rubber squeal, no kiss goodbye.
For years she sat with me beneath the trees
and hunted bearded gnomes and four-leaf clover.
But that was when she still had knobby knees
and loved her mother. Those days are over.
Remembering April, the whole world wet and green,
I pray for rain, for seven, for seventeen.

Sniper

He lifts the rifle carefully, while Death
Sits like a patient uncle. Then he squeezes
The gently yielding trigger. Half a breath
Escapes him as the tensile mainspring eases.

A bullet sings, and finds its chosen place:
An intersection where taut spider thread
Marks a right angle on a human face —
His scope reveals a flagrant burst of red

Just for an instant. Motionless he waits
Ten calibrated seconds by his watch.
Unbroken silence. Turmoil dissipates.
Tonight the stock receives a single notch.

He draws the bolt back, and a glint of brass
Hops like a praying mantis on the grass.

JOSEPH S. SALEMI

A Feminist Professor Lectures
on **The Rape of the Lock**

This is a patriarchal, sexist piece:
The lock's a helpless, victimized, ideal
Gynal trophy (like the Golden Fleece)
That masculinist enterprise must steal.
Persons without false consciousness should feel
Outrage at how Belinda is oppressed
Both by the Baron, and the author's zeal
For perfumes, *billet-doux,* and all the rest
Of hierarchy's baubles. Women dressed
In corsets, bustles, petticoats, and stays!
Such voyeuristic cameos suggest
Gender restriction more than beauty's praise.
As for the forfex — well, now there you are:
It's phallomorphic, just like Freud's cigar.

Invicti

They hauled the academics to the bar
(The legal one — not where cocktails are poured)
To answer charges brought from near and far
About a trifling, narcissistic horde
Who pettifogged and lied in ways untoward
Then chewed and spat out mangled chunks of text
In febrile fury, while their students snored.
Presiding judge and counsel, deeply vexed,
Conferred in chambers, sought out some pretext
To keep proceedings secret, lest a flood
Of testimony leave the world perplexed
And screaming for the academics' blood.
But from the dock the prisoners cried aloud:
"Our laurelled heads are tenured — and unbowed!"

Projector

I know the glints of tenderness that move
Across your face when you are close to me,
The light of shared affection, even love,
Are but projections of my fantasy,

The way a film can move us to believe
In the illusions flickering through each scene,
And make us weep or tremble, laugh or grieve,
All by a trick of light upon a screen.

Yet when you're near, the music always swells,
The lights go dim, the lion starts to roar,
And the illusion that I love so well,
Begins to play within your eyes once more;

And for that interlude, however brief,
I willingly suspend my disbelief.

Superheart

Like Superman with all his super powers,
Cruising at lightning speed around the Earth,
Or leaping from Metropolis's towers,
Or soaring toward his fortress in the north,
His mighty prowess never falling victim
To any weapon save for (strangely enough)
A fragment of his long-lost planet Krypton,
Wounded by what he could not help but love,
So I too had lately come to feel
Invulnerable, the enemy subdued,
The bullets bouncing off my heart of steel,
Safe in its arctic fortress of solitude,
Or rising up in solitary flight —
And then you came along: my kryptonite.

That Feeling of Impending Doom

You know that feeling of impending doom
Brought upon you by the late night call,
The arcane symptom, fatal (you presume),
The ambulance racing to the hospital;
Then when the ER proves unnecessary,
The shrilling phone call only a wrong number,
The symptom harmless (or imaginary),
Once more you can resume your peaceful slumber,

Reassured that family and friends
And you yourself are out of danger's way
And that the cosmic order's been put right.
But see — it's just a temporary stay.
The phone call shrilling loudly in the night —
It shrills for thee. Believe it. Doom impends.

A.E. STALLINGS

Moving Sale

How came we by this quantity of junk?
A kind of shipwreck, washed up in the yard,
Glittering cheaply in the sun: the marred,
The obsolete, redundant. We are sunk
Deep in things. That hermit crab, the soul,
Crawled up tight into its borrowed shell,
Grows attached to where it has to dwell.
The world is furnished with the physical.
But one by one, the strangers lift away
What we have touched and worn, to curse and bless
Our things to a new life of usefulness,
And we, the sunlight spent, call it a day,
And rising up at last, feel rich and strange.
It is the weight and weightlessness of change.

122

How I Learned the Poets were Right about the Sea

To me, a beach meant sandiness, and subtle
Grey gradations: sand and sea and sky.
The grains long polished by the smooth rebuttal
Of the tide, it seemed hyperbole
Of pretty poets, nothing worse or more,
To say of all that angry whispering,
Or laughter, muffled, that it was a roar,
Just as we say that birds or crickets sing.
But you took me to Brighton, where the strand
Is pebble-strewn. We stood below the pier,
All circus lights, loud stars. Here was no sand.
The surge clapped stone with stone. You held me near:
The fire-eater horizon shut his jaws,
And all around, the ocean's wild applause.

MAURA STANTON

Cubist Self-Portrait

Look at me closely. My head's a triangle,
My arms, two cylinders, my heart, a cube.
I'm spread across this space in a tangle
Of parts, reduced to bits and hollow tubes.
I'm front and back at once, androgynous,
Distorted by time into a blur of motion,
My face two spheres, my eyes so numerous
They swim around like fish in the ocean.
Once I was hidden in that little frame
Of the sonnet, genteel and decorous,
But now an X-ray reveals the skeleton
Beneath my skin, and opens me to shame.
My inner mess has now become so famous
I can't remake the whole that's come undone.

Catharsis

A busy road: I hear a high-pitched wail
Above the traffic, and I catch my breath
To see a big raccoon — masked face, striped tail —
Calling her frightened babies back from death.

The indifferent cars don't notice our panic
As they stream forward in the early twilight —
My waves and screams, her bitter bitter shriek —
As the confused cubs run toward the headlights.

I cover my face. But when I dare look up
The mother's got the babies near the culvert
Under the bridge. I watch them all drop
Into the safety of the sewer, no one hurt.

The drama's over, but I can't weep or cheer.
Have I been purged, or learned a deeper fear?

Walking Her Home

Exhilarated by the wet and wind,
He may have been too quick and droll by half,
But she was at his side and capuchinned,
And he felt cheered that he could make her laugh,
As gusts splashed water-droplets from the trees;
Though other nights would sink him to a chair,
His head bowed and his elbows on his knees,
His hands plunged in the darkness of his hair,
He folded back her hood and kissed her brow.
And that much she would never disavow.
They walked on, trading jest and anecdote;
The street was plastered leaves and chestnut burs;
His hands deep in the pockets of his coat,
She tightly hugged his arm in both of hers.

Scavenger

On failing to write a poem about Hart Crane

He gleams, a moon in water, round and bright,
that darts and drifts the way the wave requires,
but he can ply the currents like a kite.

Now, plunging under, into velvet mires,
he'll dawdle in the dungeons of excess,
a keeper of the stores — return address
unknown, of even the poet who lay his head
among the furrows, where like sea-plucked lyres
the trembling reeds ascend. If he desires
he'll turn into a stone, and playing dead,
await the feast that elegy provides.

For the crab in the iron hood, that does not weep,
knows nothing but the meter of the tides
that shunt the magic parcels to his keep.

DAVID STEPHENSON

Lazarus

After you were brought back from the dead
And the attendant uproar had died down,
Were things the same for you in your hometown?
Did you inspire involuntary dread?
Did people point and whisper when you passed?
Did women find you spooky and remote
And flee the scene whenever you approached?
Were you unhappy, lonely and outcast?

Or were you honored for the mysteries
You must have understood? Did people seek
You out to ask what being dead was like,
And did you terminate their inquiries
With answers, or with an unnerving sweep
Of eyes that flashed with otherworldly light?

Case Study

Her mother used to drink and run around;
She often had to get herself to school
Without clean clothes or breakfast, having found
Mom still asleep, locked up with some new fool.
In time Mom disappeared, and she was sent
To a pragmatic foster home, where she
Was worked like Cinderella for her rent
And made familiar with authority.

When asked about the past, she'll tell you she
Was blessed. There's nothing anyone can do
To make her brood on childhood misery.
She's doomed to the unfathomable view
That one should make the best of destiny.
To fix this would take years of therapy.

DAVID STEPHENSON

Alchemist

Since Master Philip died, I've worked alone
At our one purpose, heating countless bowls
Of lead or iron shavings over coals.
I add quicksilver, saltpeter, burnt bone,
Blood, egg yolk, arsenic, alum, and brimstone,
The base ingredients whose chemic roles
Have been deduced; then, studying my scrolls,
Some substance whose effect is still unknown.

But I have not made gold. My work has brought
Blurred vision, shaking hands, and constant aches,
The worst one in my heart. For it does seem
I'll die without achieving what I've sought,
Or even understanding my mistakes,
Or what to blame, my method or my dream.

Equator

The natives of this region built a temple
On the equator, centuries ago.
How on earth, I wonder, did they know
They'd found the heart of things, in times so simple?

The two of us were never as aware.
This photo shows us there, your palm to mine,
On either side of the imagined line,
Shadowless and hot, the laughing pair.

I know. I should have built a monument
To you; I should have learned to honor years
With stone cathedrals, though I never thought as much.

This photograph now seems a testament
That we were always split by hemispheres,
Even there, even as we touched.

HENRY TAYLOR

An Ending

At opposite ends of many of their days
one of them tiptoed as the other slept,
since they were wedded to opposing ways
of keeping such appointments as they kept.
What came of all that care is hard to know;
gold foil and compass are quaint figures for
the wayward spirals of their to and fro.
They frayed beyond the grasp of metaphor,
but once at Coolbrook, letting landscapes pass,
he watched a ripple in the antique pane
divide a horse that cropped the orchard grass
beyond the post-and-rail along the lane.
The two halves stayed in step through edgeless air,
then joined and kept on grazing, unaware.

At the Grave of E. A. Robinson

Decades of vague intention drifted by
before I brought small thanks for your large voice —
a bunch of hothouse blooms and Queen Anne's lace
and four lines from "The Man Against the Sky."
My poems, whatever they do, will not repay
the debt they owe to yours, so I let pass
a swift half hour, watching the wind distress
the fringes of my fragile, doomed bouquet.

I beg your pardon, sir. You understood
what use there is in standing here like this,
speaking to one who hears as well as stone;
yet though no answer comes, it does me good
to sound aloud, above your resting place,
hard accents I will carry to my own.

Editorial Suggestive

(From a 21st Century Editor)

"What lips these lips have kissed and where and why" —
A hot beginning! What the readers want!
But could the lips be *hips* — get more "up front"
to better wake and shock the weary eye?
Must it be ghosts that tap the glass and sigh?
Why not a well-remembered lad at the front
door? (Or, better at the back?). You won't
quite let him in, but then — No, what have *I*
to say about it? It's your poem, n'est-ce
pas? *Lain* — good verb — although the lay could be
more tempting. Set the reader's cheeks aflame.
Bend those boughs. Take him up against that tree —
out in that rain! And one more thing — oh, yes —
dear Edna, you must also change your name.

ANTHONY TUCK

Ghost

When I was eight I knew there was a ghost
that lived alone above the second floor.
He'd creak the boards and slam the old oak doors,
and I, of all my brothers, heard him most.

He might have come from church yards down the street;
our attic seemed the perfect place to haunt.
He'd scare us with his supernatural taunts
and crack the plaster in the August heat.

Later on when ghosts became more rare,
he'd hang around in boxes of old things
like crayon portraits and garnet high school rings
or maybe gently touch my thinning hair.

I haven't seen the old man recently —
my son, however, thinks he looks like me.

CATHERINE TUFARIELLO

Ghost Children

Trying to offer comfort, friends remark
How lucky it is we never had a child.
I nod agreement, knowing in the dark
They'll wake me, wild, inconsolate. You smiled
Good-naturedly when we debated names
After the wedding, wondered whether your
Features or mine would make the stronger claims —
My hazel eyes? Your hair, a black so pure
It is tinged with blue? Back home in Hawaii, you said,
Hapa children are know for special beauty.
I hoped they'd have your cheekbones, and instead
Of my pale, your golden skin. Now I mourn the pretty
Darlings I carry but cannot have, the ghost
Children whose faces are mirrors of all we've lost.

In a Season of Political Faction

The slow spring lifts its body once again
As if it were a ship swamped in a gale;
It rights itself. An avalanche of pain
Pours from its battered bows across the rail.
But every time it settles deeper in,
Its shell-like skies and petals overwhelmed:
How can the frail and fragrant jessamine
Contest the governance of a thing unhelmed?
The cold salt in its tons run everywhere,
And kills whatever is still sweet and warm:
No blossoming of fleshy peach or pear
Can coax an ounce of pity from the storm.
And now the light fades, and the hour grows late:
Over the waste blows the dark wind of hate.

Views

FIRST POET:

I fly all the time, and still I'm afraid to fly.
I need to keep both feet on the ground, the earth
within reach of my eyes. In airports I comfort myself
by assessing others — look at that handsome necktie,
the weave of that suit, the portfolio, (people of worth
are going to be on this plane) the pearls on that shelf
of expensive bosom, the hairdresser's art! All this
tells my shuddering spirit that God wouldn't tip
my seatmates, all these important people, from sight.
Once the stewardess passed the word that Liz
would be joined in Rome by Richard Burton, who was up
in First Class. I have never felt so safe on a flight.

MONA VAN DUYN

Views

SECOND POET:

I too fly all the time, and still I tremble.
I arrive too early and sit there sweating and cold.
I read at a book but can't make out what it means.
I look around at the others as they assemble
and make a collection of the dowdy old,
backpacking young, slouched in their dusty jeans,
men who have business suits of the wrong size on,
Frizzled Hair, Greasy Hair and Drooping Hem.
Humbly they live and humbly they will die —
this scroungiest bunch of people I've ever laid eyes on.
Surely God has no special fate in mind for *them,*
I tell myself, like a plane falling out of the sky.

RICHARD WAKEFIELD

Late

The neighbor man dropped dead in my front yard.
I saw him fall, I tried to think he'd tripped,
but no one tripped goes down so limp so hard,
so like a puppet when its strings are snipped.
Of course I tried my Boy Scout CPR.
I knelt, I breathed, I counted, though I could tell
the moment that I touched him I was far
too late — and he, of course, was late as well.
And later, when the ambulance was gone
and I had given his widow my sympathy,
I found within his imprint on my lawn
a misdelivered letter, late, for me,
almost directly from his hand to mine,
an invitation I could not decline.

The Calling

He's out behind the farmhouse and he's lost.
Flashlight in hand, the beam true and strong,
he looks up at the stars. The stars seem wrong.
How did he get here? He feels like he's been tossed
up by a storm, a deluge coming on.
The fog, grazing in the pasture, hunkers down.
Which way to go? Out into the darkness
with the crickets scritching their old song?

Or inward into what's been calling him:
the goldenrod, ghostly on the hill;
the yellow corn; the granary and silo growing dim;
the moonless night; the shadow, damp, and chill.
Inside, his wife begins to hum a hymn:
tonight, at least, life gathers him back in.

RONALD WALLACE

Here

And when he says that he's unpacked his bags
(as far as this life goes) does he mean
his steamer trunks of memory are empty,
his Samsonite imagination stacked
in some dusty attic where his wonder sags
like a cloth valise never to be seen
again, his shirts and shoes, his toiletries,
his underwear and hopes and hats racked

neatly in his closet? Or does he mean
he's here at last, this place he wanted to be,
the land he so long ago bought his ticket for?
And is this home? The season bursting in green?
Naked in his old age, he opens the door
and he's a tourist again. There's so much to see.

Baggage

Don't tell me you expect to find a guy
who comes with just a daypack. That's enough
to date on, maybe, but — to marry on?
You're bothered by a little freight? But why?
Give me a man who's travelling with stuff,
with serious luggage, not just carry-on —
whole skeletons in Samsonite; who brings
impedimenta — parents, kids, ex-wife,
outstanding loans. The stained and rumpled things
in steamer trunks and duffles are a life:
The more of it the better. Where you've been
and what you've brought along — if you've been far
and filled a lot of battered leather, then
don't call it baggage. It's just what you are.

DEBORAH WARREN

Grand Larcener

È amore un ladroncello.
— Così fan tutte (da Ponte)

He didn't knock. Why give himself away?
He picked the lock, assessed her — body, soul,
heart, all the valuables — and didn't stay.

Nobody saw him, or the thing he stole
— something heavy, something she won't get back —
slung on his shoulder in a purple sack.
He did replace the section he was taking
out of her chest: he cut, from an endless roll,
a length of emptiness, and filled the hole —
to delay discovery of the theft by faking
the missing part — with a batting of hollow air.

She looks quite whole; the dummy space goes on
pulsing; but, although there's nothing there,
it's heavier than the heavy thing that's gone.

Pilgrims in Assisi

Not the most perfect path to meditation —
two teachers trailed by 21 reluctant
teenagers — but we've stopped at every station
sacred to Francis, hoping the seduction
of holiness will take. The works of Giotto
have failed to make a memorable impression.
"I'm cool, don't bore me" is our students' motto
and art's another chore, another lesson.
But, framed in glass, a robe that Francis wore
brings several to a stop. They're mesmerized
by coarse brown cloth. This relic's not a bore:
its shape, its touch, is human. He's their size,
this man. His blessing settles on our days,
our unwilled poverty, our voiceless praise.

Next Week, The Sciences

The government's Department of Abolition
of Standards took on literature this week.
Our goal is universal recognition
of writers, dead or living. We must seek
equality! Perhaps you thought Jane Austen
superior to Harriet Beecher Stowe.
She might have been in 19th-century Boston,
but criticism marches on. We know
today that writers are created equal
(except for dead white European males)
and every poet's worth his salt. The sequel?
There is no canon! Liberty prevails!

"Will everyone get published and get paid?"

Watch for our guidelines on the bookstore trade.

Confessional Poem

Let me confess: I've never been abused,
poked by lascivious uncles, burned by cigarette
lighters, tied to the bed. I've never used
a drug more powerful than anisette.

It's all my fault. There's no one else to blame
for major screw-ups and humiliations,
wrecking the car, blowing the team's big game,
not living up to my mother's expectations.

There's no defense. There's no one I can sue
for wrongful birth. My horseleech egotism
is mine alone, my slothfulness, my tru-
ly ghastly writhings under criticism.

Sit back, relax, and watch my guilt expand.
It's a poet thing. You wouldn't understand.

In Trackless Woods

In trackless woods, it puzzled me to find
Four great rock maples seemingly aligned,
As if they had been set out in a row
Before some house a century ago,
To edge the property and lend some shade.
I look to see if ancient wheels had made
Old ruts to which the trees ran parallel,
But there were none, so far as I could tell —
There'd been no roadway. Nor could I find the square
Depression of a cellar anywhere,
And so I tramped on further, to survey
Amazing patterns in a hornbeam spray
Or spirals in a pine-cone, under trees
Not subject to our stiff geometries.

Fire

Imagine that first fire, the doubletakes
Among the vegans, cold, dark, wet: Cave guy
Strikes flint and, boom, you're grilling mammoth steaks,
You're holding hands, you're hooking up, you're dry,

And (years of R&D) it catches on,
Brick ovens, candlelight, of course appalling
Losses, but still, fondue, filet mignon,
And the three-alarm, fanned fire of your first calling

Until there's no more call for you, you box
Up your life's work, archive the ardencies,
The once hot, test-tube topics, and retire
To country climes, keeping an eye on the phlox
In your old field, avuncular now, at peace
With not quite having set the world
                                           on fire.

GREG WILLIAMSON

To His Love

Those poeteers were full of it, that love
Whose mood was maudlin, juvenile, and pat,
And I am far far too urbane for that,
Smiling and smirking, offering to prove
All of the pleasures I made mention of,
A glib and cocky-eyebrowed acrobat,
Because the flowers fade, the girls get fat,
And old age drops like winter from above.

But when I saw you on the brownstone stair
In blue jeans, with a flower in your hair,
More beautiful and sad than summer rain,
I fell in love with you and could not feign
The dispassionate lecher of the long weekend.
    Come live with me and be my friend.

A Brief History of the Sonnet

Sicily — Creation in the High Middle Ages:

Although its origins are generally associated with the Renaissance, the sonnet was actually created nearly 800 years ago in the late-Medieval, Sicilian court of Frederick II (1194-1250), the Holy Roman Emperor and King of Sicily. Frederick, nicknamed *stupor mundi* (the wonder of the world), was a great patron of the arts, and his Italianate kingdom extended from the island of Sicily in the Mediterranean to Naples on the Tyrrhenian Sea. To establish order in his Catholic dominions, Frederick maintained a group of fourteen legal officials called notaries at his royal court to draw up legal documents. It was in this group of Sicilian lawyers that the sonnet was first created, as Frederick's well-educated notaries passed around their creations at court. Fifty-eight of these early sonnets still survive, some quite excellent, and some reputedly written by the Emperor himself.

At least twenty-six of the fifty-eight surviving Sicilian sonnets were written by Giacomo da Lentino, later memorialized in Dante's *Purgatorio* (Canto XXIV). Although little is known about da Lentino, various scholars have speculated, without any evidence, that he created the first sonnet, and there are also many related theories about how the sonnet structure first came into being, some associating its proportions to Pythagoras' Golden Mean (despite its different 8:5 ratio) and even the Fibonacci series. The truth is, we have absolutely no idea which of Frederick's notaries first came up with the Sicilian sonnet, and it seems far more probable that its creation was a matter of "inspiration" in the course of composition (as J. L. Borges speculates in his poem *"Un Poeta del Siglo XIII"*) rather than some kind of externally-imposed mathematical construct. This is especially likely given the fact that the first eight lines (or "octave") of the Sicilian sonnet (which rhymes abababab) is essentially the eight-line stanza known as the *strambotto*, which was commonly used in Sicilian folk songs. It seems highly probable that the unknown originator of the sonnet (*sonetto*, "little song") took the *strambotto* and then added two tercets consisting of six lines (the "sestet," rhyming cdecde) to create the 14-line Sicilian sonnet.

In both subject and tone, these early sonnets set the pattern for the next two hundred years, being essentially love poems, often with a spiritual foundation. Yet despite the court's enthusiasm for these new Sicilian poems, the sonnet would not become widely known until the Renaissance.

Medieval Florence — Dante:

T. S. Eliot has written that "Dante and Shakespeare divide the modern world between them; there is no third" (*Dante*, 1929), and both of these preeminent literary geniuses found themselves drawn to the irresistible sonnet. In *La Vita Nuova* (1292), the world's first sonnet sequence, Dante Alighieri (1265-1321) composed a series of sonnets, along with supplemental commentary, that expressed his distant yet very personal and emotional love for Beatrice Portinari, a woman he'd first seen when he was nine years old and she was eight, and whom he never knew personally. Within his exquisite sonnets, Dante establishes Beatrice as his earthly ideal who, at first, causes him serious emotional difficulties, but who eventually leads him, as she will in his epic *Commedia* (1321), toward God — serving as a symbol of Christian salvation. These sonnets are deeply felt, personal and psychological, and they prepare the way for Petrarch.

In structure, Dante chooses to use the rhyme scheme reputedly adapted by Guittone d'Arezzo (1230?-1294) from the original Sicilian model. This pattern, known as the Italian sonnet (and later as the Petrachan sonnet), uses a new "enveloping" pattern in the octave, abbaabba, which creates a tighter cohesion in the first eight lines given the new central couplet which fuses the first four lines with the subsequent four and clearly establishes the octave as a seamless unit of thought. Petrarch would later follow this pattern as well, similarly using a number of variants in the sestet (usually cdecde or cdcdcd).

Francesco Petrarca (1304-1374), the greatest literary figure of the Italian Renaissance, was also the most important and influential sonneteer of all time. Unlike Dante, who is always associated with his *terza rima* masterpiece the *Commedia*, Petrarch's reputation rests entirely on his perfection of the sonnet. Petrarch's sonnets, similar to Dante's, express his distant but very real and frustrated love for a young woman he identifies as Laura, who was most likely Laurette de Noves. Given that Petrarch had taken minor orders in 1326 and that Laura seems to have been a married woman, the poems are full of deep personal frustrations. These sonnets, although they have much in common with Dante's, are generally written in a less exalted style, and, being in tune with the new Renaissance humanism, they seem even more personal. In his earlier sonnets, Laura is an ideal but very real presence who inflames him with passionate desire, but the sonnets written after her death in 1348 seem to, as with many of Dante's poems to Beatrice, envision her more as an angelic presence directing his thoughts to God.

Petrarch's mastery of the form and the popularity of the sonnets in his *Canzoniere* ("Lyric Poems") combined with the cultural excitement of the early Renaissance to make the little *sonetto* the most popular and imitated form in Italy and, in time, in all of Europe.

The European Sonnet:

In the wake of Petrarch, the sonnet, along with many other Renaissance concepts and attitudes, moved into the neighboring countries of Europe, each of which soon produced excellent sonneteers. In France, Pierre de Ronsard (1524?-1585) was the master of the Pléiade poets, and exquisite sonnets were also written by Joachim du Bellay (1522-1560) and Louise Labé (1524-1566?). In Spain, the sonnets of Juan Boscán (1490-1552) would inspire Garcilaso de la Vega (1501?-1536) and Lope de Vega (1562-1635) to write in the form. In Italy herself, the sonnet tradition was admirably carried forward by Torquato Tasso (1544-1595) as well as his earlier predecessors, Michelangelo Buonarotti (1475-1564) and Baldassre Castiglione (1478-1529). Further west, the Spanish introduced the sonnet into Portugal, the small but important explorer-nation, which produced Luís de Camões (1524-1580), the author of the last great western epic, *Os Lusiadas* (1572), as well as several hundred masterful sonnets. Camões, more than any other poet in the first four hundred years of the sonnet, expanded the little *sonetto*'s subject matter. Although most of his sonnets were love poems (including many that were quite idiosyncratic), Camões also wrote sonnets about myth, history, contemporary politics, nature, religion, and personal despair.

Europe's subsequent dedication to the sonnet can be recognized in the fact that many of her greatest poets from the Renaissance to the modern era were also distinguished sonneteers, including: Goethe, Pushkin, Baudelaire, D'Annunzio, and Mallarmé.

The English-language Sonnet:

The influence of Petrarch is clear at the very beginnings of modern English literature when Geoffrey Chaucer (1343?-1400) in his *Troilus and Criseyde* (c1385, Book I, II, 400-420) translated one of Petrarch's sonnets (#132), although Chaucer chose to render the poem in rhyme royal stanzas. The actual sonnet format would not appear in England until two hundred years later, at the beginning of its own Renaissance, when Sir Thomas Wyatt (1503?-1542) began translating some of Petrarch's sonnets using the Italianate rhyme scheme. Wyatt, in both his adaptations and his own sonnets, used the traditional Italian pattern, but he preferred the rarer sestet rhyme-scheme of cdddcc which allowed for the origins of the couplet-ending sonnet in English. Such a pattern was more clearly defined by Wyatt's friend, Henry Howard, Earl of Surrey (1517?-1547), who created what is now known as the English sonnet (or Shakespearean sonnet) — abab cdcd efef gg.

This new rhyme scheme not only allowed for many new possibilities of internal division within the sonnet (4-4-4-2, or 8-4-2, or 8-6, or 12-2, etc.), but it made composition in the more rhyme-difficult English language much easier. The new form also gave great emphasis and power to its final couplet. Generally, the structure of the asymmetrical, two-part, Italianate sonnet was seen as a situation-response format: the octave presents a problem or situation, which leads to a turn or "*volta*" in line nine where the sestet comments on or resolves the sonnet's "problem." But now the new English sonnet, with all its various possibilities of inter-nal structure (including the traditional 8-6 format) put tremendous emphasis on its concluding couplet. Since the final couplet of the English sonnet often tends to summation, or aphorism, or wit, the English sonnet was typically seen as a more "analytical" (even more intellectual) structure than the Italianate form, which tend-ed to a more "emotional" but less climatic expression. These, of course, are only basic, though useful, generalizations since both sonnet formats allow for endless possibilities and variants.

Ten years after the death of Surrey (and fifteen years after the death of Wyatt), Richard Tottel published *Songes and Sonettes* in 1557. This collection of lyrics, generally known as *Tottel's Miscellany*, contained many of the sonnets of Wyatt and Surrey, both of whom had adapted the European hendecasyllabic (eleven syllable) line into the sturdy English iambic pentameter which was presently coming into its own. Thus the pioneer sonnets of Wyatt and Surrey laid the groundwork for the great Elizabethan sonnet revival that would begin about twenty-three years after the publication of *Tottel's Miscellany*.

The sudden explosion of the sonnet at the end of the 16th Century resulted in a number of lengthy English sonnet-sequences, including Sir Philip Sidney's *Astrophel and Stella* (1591), Edmund Spenser's *Amoretti* (1595), and William Shakespeare's *Sonnets* (1609). The publication of Shakespeare's elegant, passionate, and intelligent sonnets represents a crucial moment in the history of the form, and it's fair to say that even if Shakespeare had never written his masterful blank verse plays, he would still be regarded as one of the greatest poets in human his-tory.

In the wake of Shakespeare, although the sequence format fell out of favor, the sonnet itself became the most popular fixed form in English literary history — a history replete with distinguished sonneteers who used the formats of both the English and Italian sonnets, as well as numerous variations and combinations, to create a long list of lyric masterpieces. With the exceptions of the Neoclassicists of the 18th Century (Johnson, Pope, and Dryden), who seemed suspicious of the unpredictable and inductive nature of the sonnet, the list of English sonneteers includes the names of almost all of the great writers in the history of the language, including John Donne, John Milton, William Wordsworth, Percy Bysshe Shelley, John Keats, Alfred Lord Tennyson, Elizabeth Browning, Gerard Manley Hopkins, and Oscar Wilde. Similarly, this irresistible attraction for the sonnet also manifested itself in America where excellent sonnets were written by Henry Wadsworth Longfellow, James Russell Lowell, and Edwin Arlington Robinson.

The Modern Sonnet:

Despite the 20th Century's obsession with "experimentation" and Pound's dictum to "make it new," the traditional rhymed sonnet continued, throughout the entire century, to attract the best writers in Western civilization. Even a short list is extremely impressive, if not daunting: Yeats, Valéry, Frost, Rilke, Machado, Lorca, Borges, Neruda, and Auden. As mentioned in the Introduction to this book, there was a period late in the century where the sonnet came under attack by various American writers who claimed that the poem was somehow an unwanted symbol of a restrictive past. Nevertheless, the traditional sonnet continued in the work of many distinguished poets like Richard Wilbur, Howard Nemerov, and Anthony Hecht, and now, at the beginning of the 21st Century, the little *sonetto*, nearly 800 years old, is in the throes of a great and exhilarating English-language revival.

— William Baer

Contributors

DANIEL ANDERSON lives in Murray, Kentucky. His books include *January Rain* (Story Line Press, 1997) and *The Selected Poems of Howard Nemerov* (Ohio University Press, 2003).

JOSEPH AWAD lives in Richmond, Virginia. His books include *The Neon Distances* (Golden Quill Press, 1980) and *Learning to Hear the Music* (Road Publishers, 1997).

WILLIAM BAER lives in Evansville, Indiana. His books include *"Borges" and Other Sonnets* (Truman State University Press, 2003); *Fourteen on Form: Conversations with Poets* (University Press of Mississippi, 2004); and *Selected Sonnets: Luís de Camões* (University of Chicago Press, 2005).

LISA BARNETT lives in Havertown, Pennsylvania. She is the author of *The Peacock Room* (Somers Rocks Press, 2000).

TONY BARNSTONE lives in Whittier, California. His books include *Impure* (University Press of Florida, 1999); *The Anchor Book of Chinese Poetry* (Anchor, 2003); and *The Literatures of Asia* (Prentice Hall, 2002).

WILLIS BARNSTONE lives in Oakland, California. His books include *The Secret Reader: 501 Sonnets* (University Press of New England, 1996); *Algebra of Night: New and Selected Poems 1948-98* (Sheep Meadow Press, 1999); and *The New Covenant* (Riverhead Press, 2002).

BART E. BAXTER lives in Issaquah, Washington. He is the author of *Peace for the Arsonist* (Bacchae Press, 1997) and *A Man, Ostensibly* (Egress Studio Press, 2004).

WILLIAM F. BELL lives in Lenox, Massachusetts. His work has

been published in *Poetry*, *Crisis*, and *America*.

DAVID BERMAN lives in Belmont, Massachusetts. His work has been published in *Iambs & Trochees* and *The Harvard Advocate*.

SARAH BIRNBAUM lives in New York City.

LORNA KNOWLES BLAKE lives in New York City. Her work has appeared in *The Hudson Review*, *The Connecticut Review*, and *The Crab Orchard Review*.

MARTHA E. BOSWORTH lives in Berkeley, California. Her work has been published in *Blue Unicorn*, *Poet Lore*, and *Piedmont Literary Review*.

ARTHUR BROWN lives in Evansville, Indiana. His work has been published in *Poetry*, *Arts & Letters*, and *Blue Unicorn*.

JACK BUTLER lives in Santa Fe, New Mexico. His books include *Nightshade* (Atlantic Monthly Press, 1989) and *Living in Little Rock with Miss Little Rock* (Knopf, 1993).

THOMAS CARPER lives in Cornish, Maine. His books include *Fiddle Lane* (Johns Hopkins University Press, 1991); *From Nature* (Johns Hopkins University Press, 1995); and *Distant Blue* (University of Evansville Press, 2003).

JARED CARTER lives in Indianapolis, Indiana. His books include *After the Rain* (1993); *Work, for the Night Is Coming* (1995); and *Les Barricades Mystérieuses* (1999) — all published by the Cleveland State University Poetry Center.

BRYCE CHRISTENSEN lives in Cedar City, Utah. He is the author of *Utopia Against the Family: The Problems and Politics of the American Family* (Ignatius Press, 1990).

WENDY COPE lives in Winchester, England. Her books include *Making Cocoa for Kingsley Amis* (1986); *Serious Concerns* (1992); and *If I Don't Know* (2001) — all published by Faber and Faber.

BILL COYLE lives in Boston, Massachusetts. His work has been published in *Poetry*, *The New Republic*, and *The Hudson Review*.

DESSA CRAWFORD lives in Phoenixville, Pennsylvania. Her work has been published in *Sparrow*, *Edge City Review*, and *Pivot*.

ROBERT DARLING lives in Keuka Park, New York. His books include *A. D. Hope* (Twayne, 1996) and *So Far* (Pivot Press, 2003).

ROBERT DASELER lives in Davis, California. He is the author of *Levering Avenue* (University of Evansville Press, 1998).

DICK DAVIS lives in Columbus, Ohio. His books include *Devices and Desires: New and Selected Poems 1967-1987* (Anvil Press, 1989); *A Kind of Love: New and Selected Poems* (University of Arkansas Press, 1991); and *Belonging* (Ohio University Press, 2002).

DANA DELIBOVI lives in Norwalk, Connecticut. Her work has been published in *Orphic Lute* and *Spirituality and Health*.

ALFRED DORN lives in Flushing, New York. His books include *Voices from Rooms* (Somers Rocks Press, 1997); *From Cells to Mindspace* (Somers Rocks Press, 1997); and *Claire and Christmas Village* (Pivot Press, 2002).

DOUGLAS DUNN lives in Fife, Scotland. His books include *The Faber Book of Twentieth-Century Scottish Poetry* (1992); *Dante's Drum-kit* (1993); and *The Year's Afternoon* (2000) — all published by Faber and Faber.

RHINA P. ESPAILLAT lives in Newburyport, Massachusetts. Her books include *Where Horizons Go* (Truman State University Press, 1998); *Rehearsing Absence* (University of Evansville Press, 2001); and *The Shadow I Dress In* (David Robert Books, 2004).

JANE FRIEDMAN lives in Cincinnati, Ohio. Her work has been published in *Writer's Digest* and *The Evansville Review*.

CAROL FRITH lives in Sacramento, California. Her work has been published in *The Literary Review*, *Asheville Poetry Review*, and *The MacGuffin*.

DANA GIOIA lives in Washington, D.C.. His books include *Daily Horoscope* (1986); *The Gods of Winter* (1991); and *Interrogations at Noon* (2001) — all from Graywolf Press.

D. R. GOODMAN lives in Oakland, California. Her work has been published in *Crazyhorse*, *South Dakota Review*, and *Notre Dame Review*.

R. S. GWYNN lives in Beaumont, Texas. His books include *The Drive-In* (University of Missouri Press, 1986); *The New Expansive Poetry: Theory, Criticism, History* (Story Line Press, 1999); and *No Word of Farewell: Selected Poems 1970-2000* (Story Line Press, 2000).

MARILYN HACKER lives in New York City. Her books include *Winter Numbers* (1994); *Love, Death, and the Changing of the Seasons* (1995); *Desesperanto: Poems 1999-2002* (2003) — all published by W. W. Norton.

RACHEL HADAS lives in New York City. Her books include *Halfway Down the Hall: New and Selected Poems* (Wesleyan University Press, 1998); *Indelible* (Wesleyan University Press, 2001); and *Laws* (Zoo Press, 2004).

SUSAN HAMLYN lives in London, England. Her books include *The Only Thing Untouched* (Flarestack Press, 2000) and *Quiet*

Myth (Mattock Press, 2000).

GWEN HARWOOD (1920-1995). Her books include *Night Thoughts* (National Library of Australia, 1992); *Present Tense* (HarperCollins, 1995); and *Collected Poems 1943-1995* (University of Queensland Press, 2003).

SEAMUS HEANEY, lives in Dublin, Ireland. He received the Nobel Prize for Literature in 1995. His books include *Open Ground: Selected Poems, 1966-1996* (Farrar, Straus & Giroux, 1999); *Beowulf: A New Verse Translation* (Norton, 2001); and *Electric Light: Poems* (Farrar, Straus & Giroux, 2002).

ANTHONY HECHT (1923-2004) received the Pulitzer Prize for Poetry in 1968. His books include *The Hidden Law: The Poetry of W. H. Auden* (Harvard University Press, 1992); *The Darkness and the Light* (Knopf, 2001); and *Melodies Unheard: Essays on the Mysteries of Poetry* (Johns Hopkins University Press, 2003).

AMY HELFRICH lives in Evansville, Indiana. Her work has been published in *Mississippi Review* and *The Evansville Review*.

JEFF HOLT lives in Irving, Texas. His work has been published in *The Texas Review*, *Cumberland Poetry Review*, and *Pivot*.

MATTHEW HUPERT lives in New York City. His work has been published by the *Neuronautic Press*.

MARK JARMAN lives in Nashville, Tennessee. His books include *Questions for Ecclesiastes* (Story Line Press, 1997); *Unholy Sonnets* (Story Line Press, 2000); and *To the Green Man* (Sarabande Books, 2004).

JERRY H. JENKINS lives in Louisville, Kentucky. He is the author of *2001: A Science Fiction Anthology* (Anamnesis Press, 2001).

ELIZABETH JENNINGS (1926-2001). Her books include

Selected Poems (1980); *In the Meantime* (1997); and *New Collected Poems* (2002) — all published by Carcanet Press.

CARRIE JERRELL lives in Baltimore, Maryland. Her work has been published in *Puerto del Sol*, *Acumen*, and *Hayden's Ferry Review*.

ALLISON JOSEPH lives in Carbondale, Illinois. Her books include *In Every Seam* (University of Pittsburgh Press, 1997); *Imitation of Life* (Carnegie Mellon University Press, 2003); and *Worldly Pleasures* (Word Press, 2004).

A.M. JUSTER lives in Belmont, Massachusetts. His books include *Longing for Laura* (Birch Brook Press, 2001) and *The Secret Language of Women* (University of Evansville Press, 2002).

HOLLY KARAPETKOVA lives in Cincinnati, Ohio. Her work has appeared in *The Crab Orchard Review* and *The Marlboro Review*.

X. J. KENNEDY lives in Lexington, Massachusetts. His books include *Cross Ties: Selected Poems* (University of Georgia Press, 1985); *Dark Horses: New Poems* (Johns Hopkins University Press, 1992); and *The Lords of Misrule: Poems, 1992-2001* (Johns Hopkins University Press, 2002).

LEN KRISAK lives in Newton, Massachusetts. His books include *Even As We Speak* (University of Evansville Press, 2000) and *If Anything* (WordTech Editions, 2004).

PAUL LAKE lives in Russellville, Arkansas. His books *include Another Kind of Travel* (University of Chicago Press, 1988); *Among the Immortals* (Story Line Press, 1999); and *Walking Backward* (Story Line Press, 1999).

BRAD LEITHAUSER lives in Amherst, Massachusetts. His

books include *Penchants & Places* (1995); *The Odd Last Thing She Did* (1998); and *Darlington's Fall: A Novel in Verse* (2002) — all published by Knopf.

KATE LIGHT lives in New York City. Her books include *The Laws of Falling Bodies* (Story Line Press, 1997) and *Open Slowly* (Zoo Press, 2003).

ANDREW LITTAUER lives in Princeton, New Jersey. His work has been published in *Ploughshares* and *The Sewanee Review*.

WILLIAM LOGAN lives in Gainesville, Florida. His books include *Vain Empires* (1998); *Night Battle* (1999); and *Macbeth in Venice* (2003) — all published by Penguin.

ANTHONY LOMBARDY lives in Nashville, Tennessee. His books include *Severe* (Bennett and Kitchel, 1995) and *Antique Collecting* (WordTech Editions, 2004).

AUSTIN MacRAE lives in Courtland, New York. His work has been published in *Pivot* and *Blue Unicorn*.

SAMUEL MAIO lives in Northern California. His books include *Creating Another Self: Voice in Modern American Personal Poetry* (1995) and *The Burning of Los Angeles* (1997) — both from Thomas Jefferson University Press.

AMIT MAJMUDAR lives in Cleveland, Ohio. His work has been published in the *Journal of the American Medical Association, India Currents*, and *The Plain Dealer*.

MARC MALANDRA lives in Fullerton, California. His work has appeared in *Poetry Northwest, Literature and Belief,* and *Cream City Review*.

CHARLES MARTIN lives in New York City. His books include *The Poems of Catullus* (Johns Hopkins University Press, 1979);

Starting from Sleep: New and Selected Poems (Overlook Press, 2002); and Ovid's *Metamorphoses* (W. W. Norton, 2004).

KATHERINE McALPINE lives in Eastport, Maine. Her work has been published in *Chronicles* and *The Nation*.

BRUCE McBIRNEY lives in La Crescenta, California. His poetry has been published in *America*, *The Lyric*, and *Spillway*.

SUSAN McLEAN lives in Iowa City, Iowa. Her work has been published in *Blue Unicorn*, *Iambs & Trochees*, and *The Classical Outlook*.

PETER MEINKE lives in St. Petersburg, Florida. His books include *Liquid Paper: New and Selected Poems* (1991); *Scars* (1996); and *Zinc Fingers* (2000) — all published by the University of Pittsburgh Press.

JUDITH H. MONTGOMERY lives in Portland, Oregon. She is the author of *Passion* (Defined Providence Press, 1999).

TIMOTHY MURPHY lives in Fargo, North Dakota. His books include *The Deed of Gift* (Story Line Press, 1998); *Set the Ploughshare Deep: A Prairie Memoir* (Ohio University Press, 2000); and *Very Far North* (Waywiser Press, 2002).

ALFRED NICOL lives in Newburyport, Massachusetts. He is the author of *Winter Light* (University of Evansville Press, 2004).

JOHN FREDERICK NIMS (1913-1999). His books include *The Six-Cornered Snowflake* (New Directions, 1990); *The Complete Poems of Michelangelo Buonarotti* (University of Chicago Press, 1998); and *The Powers of Heaven and Earth: New and Selected Poems* (Louisiana State University Press, 2002).

JESSICA PIAZZA lives in Brooklyn, New York.

WYATT PRUNTY lives in Sewanee, Tennessee. His books

include *"Fallen from the Symboled World": Precedents for the New Formalism* (Oxford University Press, 1990); *Unarmed and Dangerous: New and Selected Poems* (Johns Hopkins University Press, 2000); and *Sewanee Writers on Writing* (Louisiana State University Press, 2000).

CHARLES RAFFERTY lives in Sandy Hook, Connecticut. His books include *The Man on the Tower* (University of Arkansas Press, 1995) and *Where the Glories of April Lead* (Mitki Mitki Press, 2001).

JACIE RAGAN lives in Hannibal, Missouri. Her work has been published in *The Lyric*, *The Midwest Quarterly*, and *Negative Capability*.

CHELSEA RATHBURN lives in Atlanta, Georgia. Her work has been published in *The New Criterion*, *Sewanee Theological Review*, and *Pleiades*.

JOSEPH S. SALEMI lives in Brooklyn, New York. His books include *Formal Complaints* (Somers Rocks Press, 1997); *Nonsense Couplets* (Somers Rocks Press, 1999); and *Masquerade* (Pivot Press, 2004).

MARION SHORE lives in Belmont, Massachusetts. She is the author of *For Love of Laura: Poetry of Petrarch* (University of Arkansas Press, 1987).

A.E. STALLINGS lives in Athens, Greece. She is the author of *Archaic Smile* (University of Evansville Press, 1999).

MAURA STANTON lives in Bloomington, Indiana. Her books include *Snow on Snow* (Yale University Press, 1975); *Life Among the Trolls*, (Carnegie Mellon University Press, 1998); and *Glacial Wine* (Carnegie Mellon University Press, 2002).

TIMOTHY STEELE lives in Los Angeles, California. His books include *Missing Measures: Modern Poetry and the Revolt against*

Meter (University of Arkansas Press, 1990); *Sapphics and Uncertainties: Poems 1970-1986* (University of Arkansas Press, 1995); and *All the Fun's in How You Say a Thing: An Explanation of Meter and Versification* (Ohio University Press, 1999).

FELIX STEFANILE lives in West Lafayette, Indiana. His books include *If I Were Fire: 34 Sonnets of Cecco Angiolieri* (Windhover Press, 1985); *The Dance at St. Gabriel's* (Story Line Press, 1995); and *The Country of Absence: Poems and an Essay* (Bordighera Press, 2000).

DAVID STEPHENSON lives in Detroit, Michigan. His work has been published in *The Lyric, Pivot,* and *Slant.*

DAN STONE lives in Washington, D.C. His work has been published in *The Sewanee Review, Crisis,* and *Tundra.*

HENRY TAYLOR lives in Bethesda, Maryland. He received the Pulitzer Prize for Poetry in 1986. His books include *The Flying Change* (1986); *Compulsory Figures: Essays on Recent American Poets* (1992); and *Understanding Fiction: Poems 1986-1996,* (1996) — all published by the Louisiana State University Press.

DIANE THIEL lives in Placitas, New Mexico. Her books include *Echolocations* (Story Line Press, 2000); *Resistance Fantasies* (Story Line Press, 2004); and *The White Horse: A Columbian Journey* (Etruscan Press, 2004).

ANTHONY TUCK lives in Boston, Massachusetts. His work has been published in *SPSM&H.*

CATHERINE TUFARIELLO lives in Valparaiso, Indiana. She is the author of *Keeping My Name* (Texas Tech University Press, 2004).

FREDERICK TURNER lives in Richardson, Texas. His books include *Genesis, an Epic Poem* (Saybrook Publishing, 1988); *April Wind and Other Poems* (University Press of Virginia, 1991);

and *The Culture of Hope* (The Free Press, 1995).

MONA VAN DUYN lives in St. Louis, Missouri. She received the Pulitzer Prize for Poetry in 1991. Her books include *Near Changes* (1991) and *If It Be Not I: Collected Poems 1959-1982* (1994) — both published by Knopf.

RICHARD WAKEFIELD lives in Federal Way, Washington. He is the author of *Robert Frost and the Opposing Lights of the Hour* (Peter Lang, 1984).

RONALD WALLACE lives in Madison, Wisconsin. His books include *Time's Fancy* (1994); *The Uses of Adversity* (1998); and *Long for This World: New and Selected Poems* (2003) — all published by the University of Pittsburgh Press.

DEBORAH WARREN lives in Andover, Massachusetts. Her books include *The Size of Happiness* (Waywiser Press, 2003) and *Zero Meridian* (Ivan R. Dee, 2004).

GAIL WHITE lives in Breaux Bridge, Louisiana. She is the author of *The Price of Everything* (Mellen Poetry Press, 2001).

RICHARD WILBUR lives in Cummington, Massachusetts. He received the Pulitzer Prize for Poetry in both 1957 and 1988. His books include *Things of This World* (1957); *New and Collected Poems* (1988); and *Mayflies* (2000) — all published by Harcourt.

GREG WILLIAMSON lives in Duluth, Georgia. His books include *The Silent Partner* (Story Line Press, 1995) and *Errors in the Script* (Overlook Press, 2001).

Acknowledgments

DANIEL ANDERSON. "Standard Time" is from *January Rain*, Story Line Press. Copyright 1997. Reprinted with the permission of the author.
WILLIAM BAER. "Snowflake" and "Adam" are from *"Borges" and Other Sonnets*, Truman State University Press. Copyright 2003. Reprinted with the permission of the author. "Fog" is published with the permission of the author.
LISA BARNETT. "To a Mismatched Pair: A Valentine" is from *The Peacock Room*, Somers Rocks Press, 2000. Reprinted with the permission of the author.
TONY BARNSTONE. "Audit" and "Arithmetic" are published with the permission of the author.
WILLIS BARNSTONE. "Wang Wei and Snow," "If I Could Phone the Soul," and "Sirens" are from *The Secret Reader: 501 Sonnets*, University Press of New England. Copyright 1996. Reprinted with the permission of the author.
THOMAS CARPER. "Why Did The" is from *Distant Blue*, University of Evansville Press. Copyright 2003. Reprinted with the permission of the author.
WENDY COPE. "The Sitter" and "Stress" are from *If I Don't Know*. Copyright 2001. Reprinted with the permission of Faber and Faber.
ROBERT DARLING. "For Richard Wilbur" is from the October 1996 issue of *Sparrow*. Reprinted with the permission of the author.
ROBERT DASELER. "Cineplex," "First Sight," and "Men's Talk" are from *Levering Avenue,* University of Evansville Press. Copyright 1998. Reprinted with the permission of the author.
DICK DAVIS. "At the Reception" is from *Belonging*, Ohio University Press. Copyright 2002. Reprinted with the permission of the Ohio University Press.
ALFRED DORN. "In Winter Light" is from *From Cells to Mindspace*, Somers Rocks Press, 1997. Reprinted with the permission of the author.
DOUGLAS DUNN. "Native Meditation" and "Night Watch" are from *The Year's Afternoon*. Copyright 2000. Reprinted with the permission of Faber and Faber.
R. S. GWYNN. "At Rose's Range" and "The Great Fear" are from *No Word of Farewell: Selected Poems 1970-2000*, Story Line Press. Copyright 2000. Reprinted with the permission of the author.
MARILYN HACKER. "Groves of Academe" is from *Winter Numbers*. Copyright 1994. Reprinted with the permission of W. W. Norton.
RACHEL HADAS. "The Old Apartment" and "The Dead Poet" are from *Indelible*. Copyright 2001. Reprinted with the permission of Wesleyan University Press.
GWEN HARWOOD. "A Game of Chess" and "An Acrostic Birthday Greeting" are from *Collected Poems: 1943-1995*, University of Queensland Press.